Amazon Parrots

Amazon Parrots
as pets

Amazon Parrots
Pros and Cons, Care, Housing, Diet and Health.

by

Roger Rodendale

Contents

Table of Contents

Introduction

Have you ever noticed the colorful parrot on a pirate's shoulder in popular Hollywood movies? Although Amazon parrots shot to fame for being the talkative accomplice of a pirate, these birds have been accepted and loved as pets for several other reasons.

On that note, an Amazon parrot, unless very well trained, is not the best thing to put on your shoulder. These highly instinctive birds need special care and attention in order to domesticate them. After all, these are New World birds that are not genetically attuned to living with human beings.

For new parrot owners, bringing home Amazon parrots can be an interesting experience. While these birds make extremely wonderful pets and companions, training them requires a great deal of patience. You also need to try and understand the behavior of your bird to bond with it better and find a simple way to train your bird.

Since these are exotic birds, their care requirements are also quite specific. You will have to make sure that you fulfil the dietary needs of these birds and give them the right housing as well. That is how you can prevent any health issues and problems with your birds. Remember, like any bird, the Amazon parrot is also highly susceptible to diseases and infections. Taking proper care and keeping the bird active is the key to a healthy pet.

This book is ideal for beginners and experienced Amazon parrot owners. It describes in detail the origin, the various species and the history of these birds. That way, you know how the bird has evolved in human company over the years and the specific steps that you need to take in order to make your home a happy space for your parrot and its owners.

The book answers the common queries that Amazon parrot owners have. These queries have been answered after looking at similar situations among other experienced Amazon parrot owners. So, you can be sure that the information in this book has been tried and tested and will help you take good care of your beloved bird.

Amazon parrots are extremely intelligent creatures that deserve to be treated with great interest. If you are someone who can spend quality time with your bird and ensure that it gets the attention that it needs, only then should you bring one home. If you have a very busy schedule, it is a good idea to start only when you have rescheduled your routine to include your parrot in it.

Once you have done that, this book can be your companion for the rest of your journey with your parrot. Of course, this journey will be filled with excitement, several laughs and of course, companionship for a large part of your life. Hopefully, this book will make your experiences more pleasant and positive.

Chapter 1: The Amazing Amazons

Amazon parrots are New World birds that were, apparently, named by Christopher Columbus. He named the short-winged green parrots Amazon parrots. He found these birds so fascinating that he actually took one back to Europe. Since their popularity increased as pets, extensive research was carried out on this species, to discover close to 30 different species of Amazon parrots.

These birds are among the most colorful and intelligent birds in the world. They are highly entertaining because of their ability to talk and their active nature. Of course, these highly instinctive birds require owners who can be patient and understanding.

In this chapter, we will understand the origin and the behavior of these birds in the wild. It will help you get a clear picture of what this species requires. That way, you know how to plan your parrot care regime to keep them comfortable and happy.

Amazon parrots are medium-sized birds that will grow to about 12-15 inches in length as adults. These birds, however, are very heavy bodied and appear quite stocky for their size. The body of these birds is predominantly green. Different species may have various colorations and markings on their wings, head and tail. The tail of these birds is short and rounded, unlike what you would expect from parrots.

The eyes of these birds are small and beady. They have a flesh-colored ring around them. The nares or the nostrils of Amazon parrots do not have any feathers. Some species may have small tufts in this region. The coloration on the beak varies. Some birds have flesh-colored beaks while others will have black beaks. These beaks have a sharp point that can be dangerous if not trimmed properly. These birds often use the beak as a third limb to assist them in climbing and holding.

1) Types of Amazon Parrots

There are so many different types of Amazon parrots across the globe. They differ in their physical appearance and even their place of origin. According to records, there are 30 species of Amazon parrots. In this book, we will discuss the most popular types of Amazon parrots that are kept as pets.

Double Yellow Headed Amazons (*Amazona oratrix*)

These birds are also known as the yellow headed Amazon or the Yellow headed parrot. These birds are known for their talking abilities. In fact, it is the best talker among all the birds in this family. They are native to Central America and the coastal region of Mexico. The name comes from the distinct yellow forehead against the green body of the bird. These birds are very inquisitive and lively. They are known for their strange body movements such as tilting the head upside down, quickly dilating the pupils etc.

Blue fronted Amazons (*Amazona aestiva*)

The name of these parrots comes from the blue feathers above the beak that merge into shades of white and yellow. Overall, the birds are green in color. The blue coloration can vary from turquoise blue to violet blue depending upon the sub-species of the bird. These birds can come across as big show offs. They also demand a lot of attention and will tell you when it is time to eat, will expect you to greet them every time you see them and so on. These birds can also mimic and sing quite well.

Green Cheeked Amazons (*Amazona viridigenalis)*

These birds are extremely attractive and find their origins in the Northastern parts of Mexico. These birds are darker green in color and have a pale green underbody. The light green cheeks are iridescent and have a purple or lilac circle. These birds are more pleasant in comparison to all the others in the same family. They are extremely playful, therefore they are quite popular among bird owners. In fact, they are such good companions that they are known to watch television quite patiently with their owners.

Lilac crowned Amazons (*Amazona finschi)*

Dr. Otto Finsch documented this species extensively in the late 1800s. The name of the bird comes from its physical appearance. The crown is lilac in color with a distinct red coloration on the forehead and the lores. This color extends even into the neck of the bird and makes a circle around the cheeks. They are dynamic birds that are native to Western Mexico, particularly the Pacific Slopes.

Mealy Amazons (*Amazona farinose)*

This bird is also known as the mealy Parrot or the Blue crowned mealy Amazon. They are the largest among the birds in this family and can grow up to 16 inches in length. They get their name from the peculiar grey and green coloration of the feathers that makes the bird appear as if it has been dusted with some flour. The blue tail tips and the blue crown are the most distinctive features of this bird, which is mostly found in Bolivia, southern parts of Mexico and Eastern parts of Brazil.

Orange-winged Amazons (*Amazona amazonica)*

The orange-winged Amazon has a green body just like any other bird in this family. What separates the orange winged Amazon from the rest is the bright orange and blue coloration on the head and face and orange wing plumage. This coloration appears only in the adult birds. These birds are found in the northern and central regions of South America and also in a few parts of the island of Trinidad and Tobago.

Panama Amazons (*Amazona panamensis*)

Also known as the Panama yellow fronted Amazon, these birds have become extremely popular pets in the last few decades. These birds are very similar to the yellow crowned Amazon but are slightly smaller and darker in its appearance. These birds are commonly found in the western region of Panama, Colombia and the islands of Pearl and Coiba. They are extremely intelligent and inquisitive birds that are known for their talking abilities.

Red lored Amazons (*Amazona autumnalis*)

These birds have the most colorful face among all the parrots. They are also known as the yellow cheek Amazon. They are known for their pretty faces, which makes this bird a favorite among bird enthusiasts. The red lores, as the name suggests, and the contrasting yellow cheeks are brilliantly colored. In addition to being gorgeous, these birds are extremely friendly. They are native to Central America and the eastern part of Mexico. You may even find these birds in Guatemala, Honduras and Belize.

White-fronted Amazons (*Amazona abifrons*)

These are the smallest of all the Amazons. These birds are extremely playful and are known for their ability to talk. These birds are known for their large personalities. They are extremely bold and inquisitive about everything around them. They are also among the two species of Amazons that are sexually dimorphic. This means you can tell the male and the female apart. The forehead is white or yellowish in this bird, which is mostly found in Central America, Costa Rica, Belize, El Salvador, Puerto Rica, Nicaragua and the Honduras.

Yellow Crowned Amazons (*Amazona ochrocephala ochrocephala*)

These birds are very well known and look similar to most other Amazon parrots. The plumes are mostly green in color except for a distinct yellow marking on the forehead. These birds are known as the single yellow head Amazon because it is different from the double yellow headed Amazon, which has yellow coloration on the whole head and nape. These birds are also more rounded than the Double headed yellow Amazons. These birds are very smart and affectionate. They grow to become great talkers. These birds are usually found in the Central part of America and in the southern part of the Amazon basin. Some birds also inhabit Peru and Trinidad.

Yellow-Naped Amazons (*Amazona auropalliata*)

These birds are also called golden-naped Amazons. These birds have a light yellow patch on the nape of the neck. Except for that, the rest of the body is green in color. These birds are known to be a lot more obedient than other species of Amazon parrots that can be a little hard to train. They have great confidence but will listen to the commands of their owners after some training. These birds are very robust and will thrive well indoors and outdoors alike. They are native to Mexico, El Salvador, Guatemala and the Honduras.

These species of Amazon parrots are quite different in their appearance. Yet when it comes to their care and requirements, these birds are quite similar to one another. They have similar diets and housing needs. We will discuss that in detail in the following chapters. Although their individual temperament may vary drastically, their behavior in the wild is quite similar.

The next section examines in detail the origin and history of the Amazon parrots.

2) Origin and History of the Amazon Parrot

The Amazon parrot belongs to the genus *amazona* and is usually found in South and Central America. These birds are mostly seen in the neo-tropical areas. Some populations of these birds are also found in the West Indies. Here, the birds thrive in the tropical and subtropical regions. The diversity of the birds in these regions is vast, as we have already seen.

This species is named after the great Amazon river that is found in South America. However, the birds inhabit a wide variety of habitats including the savannahs, wooded forests, tropical forests and even mountains.

It is believed that these birds were discovered by Portuguese sailors. These sailors named the birds after the sound or call that they made. They were named Kriken, which is a word derived from *criquer*, a French word that translates to screech. So, now you know what to expect from your parrot!

In the 1800s, these birds were seen in scientific literature where they were first referred to as Amazon Parrots. In the book "The Speaking Parrot", Dr. Karl Russ talks about Amazon parrots as green, short-tailed parrots from America. This is one of the most notable mentions of the birds in scientific literature.

When the New World was discovered, several parrots from South and Central America were taken to Spain. From here, these colorful birds were taken across Europe. Christopher Columbus, when returning from America to Spain in the year 1492, brought back a pair of Cuban Amazon Parrots for Queen Isabella. In the 19th century, European naturalists, who were very keen on zoological interests, researched extensively and raised a lot of awareness about these birds. During this period these gorgeous birds became extremely famous among the royalty of Britain and Europe. They became popular mainly for their incredible ability to speak.

Around the 1800s these birds became so popular that people began to write several books about these parrots. However, classification of these birds was not clear as they were often confused with other green colored parrots. These birds were also not easily available back then because one had to bring them all the way from the Americas and the journey was quite arduous. Even to this day, only experienced aviculturists are able to distinguish between the different species of Amazon parrots. So one can only imagine the difficulties that researchers faced back then with limited access to these birds.

It was only around the beginning of the 20th century that more light was thrown on these birds. With the costs of crossing oceans coming down, people were able to bring back more birds. This made them available to everyone, including the educated class, sailors and even innkeepers. Other large neo-tropical parrots also became popular around this time. Of course, the birds became a lot more popular in the United States than in Europe because of the proximity of the former to the native areas of Amazon parrots. The United States shared the Mexican border, where the birds were found in abundance. This was also a simple route to import the birds into these areas.

The beginning of the 20th century saw a lot of ups and downs in interest towards large parrots because of national events. During the World Wars, parrot ownership went down drastically. In addition to that, several bird diseases broke out during that time, making it harder to keep pet birds at home.

It was only after the Second World War that things eased up, making air transport cheaper. That is when imports in exotic birds saw a steep rise. People began to favor large birds yet again. Different types of parrots including African Greys and Amazon parrots were brought to the United States. That is when captive breeding and aviculture became extremely popular. Today, there is a restriction on importing these birds because of the impact on their numbers in the wild. Captive breeding is however allowed and these parrots thrive quite well in captivity, too. As a result, Amazon parrots are available all over the globe and are extremely popular pets.

3) Taxonomy

All green parrots that are commonly referred to as Amazons belong to the genus *Amazona*. The size may range from medium to large depending upon the species of the bird. These birds are extremely stocky and are mostly green in color. The round boxy tails are typical of these birds. There are several colorful accents in these birds that help us classify one species from the other. You have a whole range as discussed above from blue, red, lilac to yellow. The colorations may be found on the wings, the tail, the head etc.

Popular naturalist Rene Lesson described these birds scientifically in the 1830s for the first time. There were several others who followed suit and described one species after another. In fact, scientists rushed forward to classify these birds so that their names could be associated with these birds. This competition became so fierce that many named species of Amazon birds without checking for any evidence or providing any specimens. This lead to a lot of confusion when classifying these birds.

Today, these birds have been better reviewed and several modifications are being made regarding their classification. For instance in the year 1991, the Committee of Classification and Nomenclature of the American Ornithologists Union suggested that the *ochrocephala* group should be reclassified. After this, only the yellow crowned Amazon was recognized under the Amazona *ochrocephala*. The other birds such as the Yellow-naped and Yellow-headed parrots have been classified differently.

Currently, there are close to 31 species of Amazon parrots according to the IUCN Red list of Threatened Species. Six of these 31 species are listed as endangered today. Another 4 species are supposed to be very close to extinction. This is one of the primary reasons why captive breeding is permitted in most countries, with pet trade being completely banned.

There are several other threats that these birds face because of their popularity. The next section discusses the conservation status of these birds to make sure that you are only bringing a bird home legally.

4) Conservation Issues

Parrot trade is an extremely lucrative enterprise that has attracted several groups to capturing and exporting these birds. As the numbers of these parrots began to fall drastically in their natural environment, several laws were structured to prevent or prohibit parrot trade altogether. However, even today, there are so many illegal sectors of the pet trade market that operate.

During the 1970s and '80s, the United States of America became a huge market for different species of parrots from across the globe. An estimated 150,000 parrots were smuggled into the country every year. To prevent this, the Wildlife Conservation Act was formed in the year 1992. This protected several bird species from illegal trade. According to this act, you can import wild birds into the country only if they have been approved for sustainable use for research and other purposes. After this Act was passed, the number of birds traded into the country reduced to just a few hundreds every year. Of course, illegal trade occurs even today, with Mexico accounting for the maximum number of birds smuggled every year.

The Defenders of Wildlife is an active group that is actually a non-profit organization in Mexico. They provide all the statistics for international parrot trade. According to their latest comprehensive study, a whopping 65,000-75,000 birds are captured every year solely for pet trade. These alarming numbers resulted in the formation of the Convention on International Trade which protects all the endangered species of Amazon parrots from being traded in an international market.

The European Union, too, participated in a temporary ban on the import of these birds. This measure was taken because several birds that were imported actually died from H5N1 flu. This ban was made permanent in the year 2007 and only a few countries are allowed to import the birds into Europe today.

Despite these laws, parrot trade remains a low risk criminal act. Since the rewards are so large, parrot trade remains the number one threat to the numbers of these birds in the wild.

There is no means to intervene and effectively solve this issue because of the lack of information on this subject. Governments across the globe do not have enough records about the different species of parrots.

Today, only one report that was made in the year 2006 by Cantu is available to understand the status of parrot trade in Mexico. This report is solely based on several interviews that were conducted with union leaders and bird traders. This document does not have any concrete evidence that can help one understand the number of birds that are being traded annually from different parts of the world. Since there is no scientific data available, a lot is left to speculations.

In addition to this, the financial limitations of organisations like the Wildlife Administration agencies makes it harder to actually conduct research on this subject and find a solution to the depleting numbers of these gorgeous creatures.

A few alternatives have been suggested, however. According to a report published in 2011 by Pires and Moreto,, crime prevention may be the only answer. This involves the identification of areas where the issue is predominant. In these areas simple measures like being a little more careful during breeding and mating seasons, closing pet markets and even installing CCTV cameras have been suggested as effective measures.

Another report by Pires and Clark states that making parrots a matter of pride for Mexico and other countries can reduce the rates of trafficking quite drastically. However, the diversity of the species available and the lack of interested urban population does not allow proper execution of this particular plan.

Investing in eco-tourism may be one of the best solutions to the issue of parrot trade. The locals getting involved with the government to cater to the large number of tourists who would flock in to see the birds makes it a viable option. That way, it would be possible to decrease the number of trappers as well. It is possible that those who trap the birds just to support their needs would switch to eco-tourism as a more lucrative option.

Besides pet trade, habitat loss is also a major threat to Amazon parrots. In some places these birds are even considered as pests because they invade the agricultural areas and damage crops like maize. Most of the species of these birds are, sadly, marked as threatened. So it is up to you to make sure that you are only investing in a legitimate breeder or pet store that does not indulge in any trapping and selling of these wild birds. If you do come across any such trader, you could report it on the websites of any of the organizations mentioned above.

5) Behavior

Amazon parrots are New World parrots that have been identified to have very strong personalities and behaviors. These birds can be really picky about the species that they share their natural habitat with. In fact, Amazon parrots may not even willingly share their space with other breeds of parrots unless they do this out of some sort of need. Their behavior has intrigued several researchers, providing us with a lot of information about the social habits, the general temperament and attitude of these birds. Here are some behavioral aspects of Amazon parrots in general:

- **They are diurnal:** This means that these birds will want to feed early in the morning. In the wild, they will wake up before sunrise and fly off to obtain food as the sun begins to rise. At dusk, they will stick to the trees that they are roosting in. Among New World parrots, the only probable exception to this rule is the Pantagonian Conure, which remains active at night. The levels of activity of this bird become even more pronounced when there is a full moon.

- **Diverse habitats:** This is one of the many reasons why these birds can be considered highly robust and hardy. They can thrive in a variety of habitats ranging from train forests to open savannahs. Sometimes, you will also find these birds in the cracks of limestone cliffs. In fact, the diversity in habitat has often put aviculturists in a dilemma when it comes to making generalizations about these birds.

- **Great resilience:** If you plan on bringing home Amazon parrots, you need to know that these birds are naturally very resilient, be it emotionally or physically. The personalities of these birds are so strong that they even seem to be too full of themselves sometimes. The temperament of these birds can range from mild and timid to even phobic birds. This usually happens when they share their home with other species of parrots like African greys. Of course, when they are sick or injured, their personality may seem a little different too. Normally, Amazon parrots are not fearful. If you see this behavior in your bird, it may be related to the health of the bird. In several cases, it has been observed that the bird develops serious conditions like Psittacine Beak and Feather Disorder after a sudden bout of phobic and isolated behavior.

- **May have multiple behavioral disorders:** Amazon parrots are highly intelligent creatures. Because of this, they may try to control you through behaviors like biting and screaming. It is necessary for the owners to be patient while training Amazon parrots. You will have to make sure that these birds are very well cared for. In fact, if they are neglected or traumatized, they may resort to extreme behaviors such as feather plucking as well. Of course, if a normally happy bird turns sour, it could be a sign of poor health or sickness of some sort. That is when veterinary attention is a must.

It is not common for Amazon parrots to develop feather plucking before they become sexually mature. In case your bird develops this condition, you may also have to revise the diet that you are following for your bird. It could also stem from hygiene issues that we will discuss in detail in the following chapters.

- **Prefer to live in flocks:** In their natural environment, these birds thrive only in flocks. They are highly social creatures that live and move with their flocks. They are collectively aggressive against other species of birds that they view as competition or threat to their well-being. Some Amazons are more aggressive than others. They have an aggressive body language, at least, with their feathers being puffed up at the sight of an intruder. These birds also strut and scare away these intruders because of their body language. This body language is also a sign for owners to back off and just leave the bird alone. If you try to pick up a bird whose feathers are erect, be sure that you will be attacked. However, the fact that they are loving towards their flock is a hint that you should try to make the a part of yours by spending more time and energy on them.

- **They can be loud:** These birds can scream really loudly. This is not to scare someone away or to show distress. It is usually only a means for them to communicate. If you let your parrot scream or if you respond in a way that the bird wants you to, screaming will become your bird's tool for manipulation. So, be very careful. They are highly vocal birds with specific calls that you will learn to respond to effectively as you spend more time with your bird.

In the end, these are only generalizations about parrot species. These birds are very unique and will come with a very strong individual personality. It also depends upon the care that these birds receive and the amount of time that you are willing to spend with them. The more you are able to learn about your own bird's unique personality, the more likely you are to meet their needs. Just remember to focus on your bird from day one and try to make them feel as welcome in your home as you can. If the housebreaking process is successful, you have overcome the biggest hurdle.

Chapter 2: Selecting Your Parrot

The first thing you need to do is find a breeder or a pet store where the birds are reared in captivity and not illegally imported. There are some common sources that you can bring your birds home from. However, whatever source you choose, make sure that the birds are kept in good condition and are, most importantly, not sold illegally. This can lead to penalties of up to $110,000 if you are not careful about it. Here are some dos and don'ts when it comes to bringing home a bird:

1) Finding a Breeder

In the recent past, several breeders have come under fire for being extremely insensitive with their breeding practices. Some have even gone to the extent of removing the hatchlings from nests and selling them off to several pet stores. This is very much like the puppy mills that are considered extremely cruel. You will be able to tell whether a breeder is genuine or not based on the care that is given to the birds. Those who only have commercial interests will most likely be extremely negligent and will keep their birds in filthy conditions. One such breeding operation that was carried out in Washington was even described as a parrot concentration camp. The birds were made to live in conditions that were too cold, damp and filthy.

Here are some reasons why it is actually your responsibility to make sure that you choose a good breeder to source your pets from:

Badly bred birds are susceptible to disease

Birds that are kept in very unhygienic conditions often suffer from several communicable diseases including proventricular dialation disease. This leads to weight loss, regurgitation and depression. These birds can transmit diseases not just to other birds but human beings as well. You can contract diseases like salmonellosis, chlamydiosis, E.coli infection, giardiasis, tuberculosis and many others. It is also very hard to care for a bird that is unwell.

Your bird could be smuggled

Almost everyday, stories of birds being smuggled are revealed. The instances in which these birds are smuggled can be really cruel. They are dumped in air vents of a vehicle, in jacket pockets etc. The industry of smuggling treats these beautiful creatures as mere commodities of trade. If you end up buying from someone who smuggles the birds in, you are supporting the industry too.

Birds are left in the lurch sometimes

With many new and inexperienced breeders, having birds becomes very overwhelming for them. As a result, they may even abandon the birds or even resell them. This is one of the many reasons why animal shelters have several parrots available for you to adopt. Close to 85% of pet owners and breeders will give their birds away because they are unable to keep them. In many states, birds are protected by a strict law of abandonment to make sure that they are not just left out of the cage when owners are unable to take care of them. You see, in captivity, birds do not belong to their natural environment, so releasing them like this leads to death and severe injuries due to unexpected predators.

Finding a good breeder

Not all breeders are commercial and unreliable. Some of them do a lot of research about finding the best breeding practices for their birds. They make sure that their clients get nothing short of the best when it comes to the quality of the birds. Here are a few things that you need to look out for when you are buying a parrot from a breeder:

Behavior of the birds: Amazons are among the most inquisitive and curious birds in the world. If you notice that the birds in the aviaries are slow to respond, fatigued and dull, it means that they are either unhealthy or lonely and bored. Good breeders will not let their birds go through either one of these stages.

The appearance of the birds: Parrots usually preen themselves well and keep their feathers well groomed. If you see that the feathers are out of place and matted in places, especially near the cloaca, it is a warning sign. Bald patches when it is not molting season is an indication that the bird may have a feather plucking disorder. The beak and the toes should not have any deformities and irregularities. They should be clean, free from scales and dirt. Amazon parrots are stocky birds. Instead, if you see that their bodies are too thin and fragile, it is sign of poor breeding practices.

The condition of the cage: Bird cages should be cleaned out on a daily basis. If not, they tend to become very smelly and dirty. If you see bird poop and feathers on the floor of the cage and if the toys are covered in bird poop, it means that basic hygiene practices are missing. Take a look at the food and water containers. If the water is murky and full of poop or feathers, the bird may not be well taken care of. This also makes the birds potential carriers of several diseases that affect people and other birds in your home. The bird that you take home may look healthy but could develop difficult health problems in the future. Be very careful about only choosing birds that are housed in very clean conditions.

Recommendations: If the breeder that you chose is reputed, he/she will have several people who will give you positive testimonials and recommendations. Your breeder will also be willing to connect you with his or her clients if they are breeding good quality birds. You can even visit their clients and talk to them about the challenges of raising a bird and the assistance that the breeder will provide you with during this course

Interest of the breeder: The way your breeder talks to you or interacts with you shows their interest in the bird. Is he/she just trying to make a sale or is he/she genuinely interested in getting the bird a good home for the rest of its life. A good breeder will try to make sure that you are competent enough to take care of the

birds that they raised with so much care and caution. Some questions that you can expect from the breeder are:
- Have you had any birds in the past? Which ones?
- How much do you know about Amazon parrots?
- Do you have any other pets in your home?
- How will you ensure that your birds get the right diet?
- What is your schedule like? Will you be able to give your bird any time at all?
- Are you aware of the potential household hazards for Amazon parrots such as heavy metal poisoning?
- Is your family ok with having a bird? Are there children in the household?

These questions will tell the breeder about your commitment to the bird and whether an energetic bird like the Amazon parrot is good for your home or not. On the other hand, if the breeder is only interested in selling you the prettiest and most expensive bird, it is time for you to look elsewhere.

2) Pet stores for Amazon purchase

Good quality pet stores are not a myth. Some of them are run by passionate individuals who are interested in breeding certain Amazon parrot species. They may be interested in increasing awareness about these birds and the joy of having them as pets. You will know that a pet store could be buying from commercial breeders or, even worse, illegally smuggling it with the following signs:

The aviary is extremely noisy: Amazon parrots stay close to their flocks in the wild. They need the companionship of their flock mates for their well- being. When they are separated from this flock after being captured, they still call out to them very loudly. For several days after they are separated from their flock, these birds continue to cry out to their birds.

Loneliness is one of the biggest issues with birds like the Amazon parrot. Besides becoming very noisy, these birds can become aggressive and could even develop issues like feather plucking.

That is when the birds begin to look unhappy and unkempt. In a good pet store, birds are usually bred in captivity. They are close to their flocks or sometimes even their parents. If the bird has no flock mate, the owners and the employees in the store take the additional effort to become their flock by spending a lot of time with them and keeping them mentally and physically active.

The birds are afraid of people: Pet stores that care for the well-being of their birds will spend a lot of time with them to make sure that they feel loved. Quite obviously, these birds are very well socialized and will be more approachable. On the other hand, if the birds have been smuggled in or have not been given the attention that they need, they will be aggressive or afraid. Most often, birds that have been smuggled in will see people as a threat to their well-being. As a result, when you approach their cage or try to interact with them, they may just retreat to a corner of the cage. Some of them become defensive and will puff up their feathers or nip at you as an attempt to scare you away. These are the signs that tell you that the bird may be a difficult one to bring home as you will have to deal with several behavioral problems.

The employees have no clue about the birds they are selling: Talk to the employees at the pet store. It is not enough for just the pet store owner to have all the information about the birds. The caretakers will be aware of the routine and the requirements of the birds if they have been interacting with them regularly. On the other hand, if they have to work with new species that are just smuggled in or bought from breeders, they may not be able to provide any information about the birds to you.

Casually enquire about the diet, the grooming process and other care requirements of the bird. Ask where the bird originates from and other questions about the species. If there is a lot of hesitation with respect to answering your queries, you need to understand that the caregivers have no experience.

The birds are kept in poor conditions: The conditions of the cage are very important for you to understand how they have been raised. A dingy and dirty cage is definitely a sign that the birds are not kept in the best conditions. However, in the case of pet stores, the bigger issue is overcrowding. Pet stores tend to just keep throwing new birds into the cages or aviaries. They take very little care about quarantining the birds as well.

This means that birds are at risk of infections, diseases and of course behavioral problems. Amazon parrots, especially, can dislike the idea of having to share their space with other birds. That means that they will retreat completely or will become extremely aggressive.

Birds catch infections really easily. If the cage is already unkempt and the birds are crowded into these cages, you know that these birds may not be the best addition to your home unless you are able to take extra care of them.

3) Guarantees for your Amazon Parrots

Whether you are getting your bird from a breeder or a pet store, insist on getting a health guarantee. Normally, pet stores may not give you this health guarantee or certificate but every reputable breeder will offer you a health certificate for the pet that you purchase, whether it is a parrot or any other animal.

A health certificate basically assures the owners that the birds are free from any disease or possible pathogens at the time of purchase. However, in case any disease or health problem occurs in the bird, it will be exchanged for a healthier one or the money is returned to the owner. The guarantee period varies from 15 to 90 days depending upon the species and the source that you obtain your bird from. There are a few conditions that you will have to fulfil in order to make sure that your health guarantee is valid for that period:

You need to get a Certificate of Veterinary Inspection for your bird with 72 hours of purchase. It is recommended that you take your bird to a licensed Avian vet. It is best that you avoid any vet that is suggested by the breeder. These vets could be linked to your breeder. If any issue is detected in this examination, your bird is exchanged immediately or a full refund is given to you.

In case you have any other bird in your home, you need to get a medical certificate and the medical history of these birds. They all need to be in good health for your guarantee to be valid.

If you notice any symptoms of disease in the bird, you must make sure that it is examined by a vet within 72 hours of the onset of these symptoms.

In case the bird dies, you need to make sure that a necropsy is performed by an Avain vet. This should be complete with a histopathy report that is made within 72 hours of the death of the bird. In case these tests prove that the bird died of congenital conditions that occurred before the sale of the bird, your money will be refunded. The bird should not be frozen after it is dead for these tests to be valid.

Normally, health certificates are not issued when the birds are shipped. This is because the process of shipping puts the birds at risk of exposure to toxins and infections. Therefore, it is best that you do not make a purchase from online stores. Unless you have recommendations from people who have interacted on a personal level with these breeders, it is always a risk as you do not really get to explore the conditions that the bird has been raised in.

The best kind of breeders are the ones that follow a closed aviary concept. This concept ensures that no birds other than the ones bred on the farm are allowed there. The birds are not even taken to pet shows where they may catch an infection from other birds. This is a great preventive measure to prevent the chance of any disease in your bird.

You also need to make sure that you take good care of the bird to prevent any health issues. Most often your breeder will be able to help you with tips and information regarding proper care. Make sure you pay attention to this. Keep upgrading your knowledge about your bird to be in touch with latest trends in care and medicine that will make your bird live a longer and healthier life.

4) Important Parrot Laws

Parrots are exotic birds in the United States, UK, Australia or any part of the world outside their natural environment. We have already established that these birds have strict import and export laws attached to them. Now, even when it comes to owning a bird that has been bred in captivity, there are various regulations that you need to be well aware of. Here are a few things that you need to keep in mind to legally have a parrot in your household:

Does it require a bird owners' license?

In some parts of the world, getting a bird owners' license is a must. If you are unsure, you can call your local wildlife authorities and make sure that you fulfil the license requirements, if any. In Australia, a bird owner's license is mandatory. You are required to get a license from the Office of Environment and Heritage to make sure that the species of bird that you are bringing home is being monitored properly. In fact there are two classes of licenses in Australia. Class 1 license allows you to keep birds that are commonly found in this region and are easy to take care of. Class 2 license is a must for rare species that require additional care. The birds belonging to each class are mentioned in detail. In addition to this, the license is only given to an individual who is 16 years of age or older. Any bird that is kept without the necessary license can be taken away from your home.

Does your lease allow you to have a bird?

Most people do not check their lease or rental agreement before they bring a pet home. This can lead to a lot of unnecessary conflict. If your lease says "no pets", you cannot bring a parrot home. It is possible that your landowner will have you evicted for breaching this legal contract. If you are discovered with a parrot or any other pet, you will be given a month's notice to leave the place.

There are a few exceptions, though. Sometimes, the landowner is aware of the existence of the pet and may not really enforce the no pet clause. This is when you can look for the three month rule which says that if you had a bird in your home for three months or more and the landlord did not enforce the rule, you can continue to stay there with your pet.

Of course, you can speak to your landlord before you get a parrot. Sometimes, the no pet clause may only refer to animals like dogs and cats and not birds. They may put down conditions like the bird will have to be removed if it is too noisy. You have to make sure that you adhere to these conditions if your landlord is letting you keep a pet despite a "no pets" clause in the agreement.

Do your neighbors have a say in this?

Yes, they definitely do. If you bring home a bird that is way too noisy and keeps screeching all day, your neighbors can object to you having a pet at home. Many bird owners have had to face their neighbors and even lawsuits for ignoring complaints about their pets. In fact, in the United States alone, there are over 100 attorneys who are working on pet-related lawsuits. Although most cases involve horses and dogs, there are times when birds are involved too.

In fact, poorly trained parrots may bite people who visit or may cause injuries to children or other pets. The affected person can and in most cases will sue you. If you lose these cases, you will have to bear all the medical expenses of the aggrieved individual along with paying him or her some reimbursement for the inconvenience caused by your pet.

Are there any limits on how many birds one can have?

In several cities, there are zoning laws that determine how many pets you can own. This law generally does not apply to birds kept indoors. However, it is a good idea to check before you take a chance. If you plan on keeping your birds outdoors, you need to check if this is allowed in your city or not.

Zoning rules apply even to breeders. Remember that birds are a large investment. If you do not check about the number of birds you can have, you may lose your birds and the aviary. That is a big investment down the drain. In addition to that, if you are unable to maintain your birds, you may even have to cough up penalties for letting them get too noisy or smelly.

Usually, a municipality may restrict the number of birds or pets in an average household to five. This also depends on the space available for the animals and several other factors that ensure the well-being of your animal or bird as well as that of the people who are sharing the neighborhood with you.

These laws about companion animals are enforced by the county or the city. So, these laws may vary tremendously from one place to another. In fact, in some states and cities, there are rules about burying your dead pet in the backyard, too. You cannot have a pet buried in city limits and will have to look for a pet cemetery. These rules include birds of all species as well.

Therefore, when you bring home a bird like an Amazon parrot that is very protected by the law, it is necessary for you to understand other smaller regulations that determine their status as pets. That way, you will not have to deal with problems like eviction or having your pet taken away from you.

5) Things to know before adopting a parrot

Parrots can be quite a handful. Not everyone is able to meet the demands of these birds. As a result, several parrots are abandoned or surrendered each year to rescue homes and bird adoption centers. If you are looking at bringing a parrot home, it would be a great idea to actually adopt one instead of buying one. Not only is this cheaper, it is also a very noble thing to do.

You can check for local rescue homes on the Internet. There are several organizations that specialize in bird adoption. Find one that offers classes and help to teach new pet owners how to take care of the birds that they plan to take home.

When you go to a shelter, check for the quarantining process that they follow. Most of them will have the birds quarantined for 30 days and will also have them examined by a certified Avian vet.

Following that, these birds will go through extensive rehabilitation where the volunteers in the shelter will ensure that the birds are properly socialized. Some of them may even appoint a trainer to teach the birds skills like stepping up.

If you plan to adopt a bird, it is recommended that you spend some time at the rescue home with these birds, try to socialize with them and pick one that suits your temperament the best. In fact, many shelters have a few mandatory hours that potential adopters will have to spend with the birds before adopting them.

Rescue shelters know best that raising birds is not that easy. Most of them will only give the birds away to owners who are well educated about parrot care. To help you develop a positive relationship with your bird, they have several free classes about health and nutrition for birds, general information about parrots, training the birds and several other important aspects of having a bird at home.

Just like the adoption of a human baby, adopting a parrot is also a lengthy process. If you do not meet all the requirements stated by the organization, you may even be denied the opportunity to take a bird home. Here is the step by step adoption process:

The application for adoption should be completed and provided on file.

6 months before adoption, you must have attended at least two classes offered by the shelter. If your parrot has been abused or has certain behavioral issues, the rescue shelter may ask you to attend more classes as well.

You should visit your bird at least 3 times before you apply for adoption. Your interaction with the bird is monitored to see if you need any more coaching and help.

If you have other birds at home, they need to be examined by an avian vet and should test negative for psittacosis.

The cage should be approved by officials from the adoption agency.

An adoption fee of $325 or £150 should be paid. This includes all the medical expenses and the food supplied to the bird until adoption. Some shelters may not charge these fees if they are funded or government aided.

If you are located more than 150 miles away from the shelter, you will have to drop a special request. This is because the home visit requirements are harder to fulfill if you live far away.

There are a few adoption policies that you need to stick to. If an official home visit discovers that you have breached them, the bird will be taken away. Here are a few policies that are common to most rescue homes:

Adopted birds should not be bred.

Birds should never be taken outdoors without a proper harness or cage.

These birds cannot be sold to another person under any circumstances. This may lead to heavy penalty if discovered by the rescue shelter officials.

The environment that you provide should be 100% smoke free. Adopted birds should be examined annually by an approved avian vet.

The diet should be well-rounded consisting of fruits, vegetables, pellets, nuts and grains.

You cannot give the bird away to someone else if you are unable to take care of it. The bird must be returned to the rescue shelter if there is any issue with keeping it in your custody.

Some of these rescue shelters may not allow you to take a parrot home if you have an aggressive pet dog or cat at home. Some of them do not allow birds in homes with children either. This is to ensure the safety of the child and the bird.

In a period of 12 months, you cannot adopt more than 2 birds. This is to ensure that you do not overcrowd your home with birds you are unable to care for.

Chapter 3: Preparing for an Amazon Parrot

For a new parrot owner, the experience can be very overwhelming if you are not prepared. Amazon parrots have a life span of 25-30 years depending upon the species. Once you have made a commitment, you need to make sure that you can sustain it for that long. Giving your parrot away after keeping it for a few years can be extremely traumatizing for the bird. They tend to form bonds quickly and get really lonely when they are separated from their family.

1) Are you ready for an Amazon Parrot?

Most pet owners make the mistake of thinking that getting a bird is as simple as just putting it in a cage, petting it and feeding it from time to time. However, there is a lot more to the bird than just that. Here are a few considerations that you need to make before you actually bring a bird home:

Why do you want the bird?

This is one of the most important questions to ask yourself. Amazon parrots are beautiful birds. More often than not, people get carried away due to the appearance and want to have one at home. A parrot is a highly intelligent creature that demands a lot of care and attention. If it is merely a commodity or a beautiful addition to your home, do not think of investing in one.

If you are planning on bringing the bird home as a companion to your child, you need to be prepared to take good care of it too. While simple activities like feeding can be taken care of by your child, you will have to do the majority of the work including training, grooming and engaging the bird. In fact, it is not recommended for you to give the responsibility of a bird like the Amazon parrot to a child younger than 12 years of age. It is not advisable, with the safety of the child in mind.

Are you prepared for the time these birds demand?

An Amazon parrot can be really playful and social. They need to be trained and entertained to make sure that they are healthy. You will also need to learn how to handle them properly in order to avoid any behavioral issues sprouting from that.

Now, most of you may think that if you have a beautiful and spacious cage for the bird, it is good enough to keep them happy. Well, think again. These birds need some time outside the cage as well. This is necessary for them to also form a strong bond with the family that they are living with.

You need to spend time with your bird to also make sure that you understand his or her behavior properly. You need to be able to tell the slightest deviation from what is normal. It is a known fact that parrots are great at hiding their illness. They will show very minute signs in the initial stages of illness. If you are inexperienced and have not spent enough time with the bird, you will just not notice it.

Do you like cleaning?

If you have a parrot at home, expect to do a lot of cleaning. A parrot who isn't messy is a myth. They poop around the clock, will make a mess while eating and will even leave a lot of feathers around from time to time. If you are not prepared to clean the cage at least once every day, wash the food and water bowls daily and even mop or vacuum your house on a daily basis, reconsider your choice of bringing home a bird. Remember, even "potty trained" parrots will have accidents because of the frequency with which they have to go. These birds have a rapid metabolism that can become somewhat of an issue for most new parrot owners.

Can you afford it?

Here is a quick breakdown of the costs involved with an Amazon parrot:

Cost of the bird: $750- $1500 or £300- 800

Housing costs: $400-1000 depending upon the size

Cost of food: $30- 60 per month

Cost of toys: $20- 40 per month

Veterinary care: $50 to 75 per visit and about $1200 annually

Miscellaneous costs: $30

So you can expect an initial investment of $1000- 1800 or £500-1000 and recurring costs of $250-300 or £100-150 every month. Keep this recurring amount aside from your monthly budget for 3 months and see if you are able to run your own life comfortably with the remaining money.

When it comes to costs like veterinary care or food, you cannot make any compromises. So, when you make the commitment, be extremely certain that you can handle the financial pressure of having one at home.

In order to prepare for a parrot, you can do the following:

- Take an Amazon parrot under foster care for a while. You could take a friend's parrot or even request a rescue shelter to help you with this. They may allow you to go to the facility and take care of the bird for a while.
- Carefully research about the species that you plan on bringing home. Understand exactly what the bird needs and how you can ensure complete care for the bird.
- You can join online forums or even local communities that work towards spreading more knowledge about pet birds and parrots. This will help you gain a lot of insight into proper care for the bird.

Once you have determined whether you are ready to bring a bird home or not, you can pick the source to get your bird from. If you are an inexperienced parrot owner, do not bring home an injured or abused bird. While it seems like a very noble thing to do, you will only do more harm than good to the bird if you are unable to provide him or her with the care that they need. Your bird will go through various stages like molting, health issues, behavioral changes etc. that you need to learn how to handle perfectly.

2) Housing preparations

You need to figure out where you will house the bird before you actually bring one home. You cannot scamper around later on to find a good cage for your bird. Complete this set up with all the toys and food or water bowls that are required. That way, your bird's first day at home will be a lot more comfortable. You will also find it simpler to let the bird into his new home instead of shifting him around when he is still trying to settle into a new space.

a) Housing considerations

Housing is a highly neglected aspect of bird care. In fact, most people just leave their birds in the transfer cage that they got at the breeders. However, the cage is more than just an enclosure. It is your bird's territory. So, the more you work towards making your bird comfortable there, the better their health will be. In fact, keeping a bird in a cage that is too small will qualify as abuse.

The first question is how large should the enclosure be? For amazon parrots, the minimum dimensions of a cage are 90-135 cms. However, if you can afford to buy a larger cage, do so. In fact, pick up the largest cage in the budget that you have set aside for the cage.

The size of the cage depends on what you plan to keep inside the cage. You do not want to add so many toys that your bird is just not able to move around. If you want to give your parrot the luxury of several toys, make sure that you also have a cage large enough to house them with the bird.

How do you ensure safety for your bird in the cage? When you buy a large cage, one important thing to consider is the bar spacing. If it is too much, your bird may just wriggle out of the cage. If it is too small, the bird may try to wriggle out and get his/her head and body stuck there. For a bird like the Amazon parrot, the ideal bar spacing would be about a $3^{rd}/4^{th}$ of an inch.

The next important thing is the material used to make the cage. Powder-coated cages and steel cages are idea. These enclosures are able to withstand your Amazon parrot's beak power. If the cage is made of poor quality material, the bird will break or bend the bars easily.

Lastly, when you buy the cage, run your hand all around the insides of the cage. If the cage is cheaper, chances are that the finish is not that great. There could be several sharp edges that may injure your bird. In addition to that, you will also hurt yourself whenever you try to clean the cage. Even rough edges or patches should be avoided as it can cause a lot of irritation for the bird if the wing or any other body part touches it.

b) Styles of cages

Bird cages can be aesthetic additions to your home. There are so many different styles that you can choose from. Depending upon the behavior of the bird and your personal needs, you can choose the type of cage that you will bring home. The common styles available are:

Open top enclosures

As the name suggests, the cage opens from the top. You can add a perch to this open end to allow your birds to perch and get a good view of their home. They can even enter the cage easily whenever they want water or food. This style is not suitable for birds that are not trained to step up as you will not be able to get the bird out of the perch to put them back in the cage and close it for the night. Of course, this type of enclosure is of no use when you have a pet cat or dog at home as you can never leave the cage open with the perch.

Playtop enclosures

These playtop cages come with a detachable top that you can even use to train your bird. They are similar to the perch of an open top cage. The difference is that the entrance to the cage is in another place. It could be at the front or the side of the cage. Once your bird has been trained, it is a great space for your bird to play and stretch.

Solid top enclosures

These are the most common types of enclosures that you will find. The top of the cage does not open and cannot be used as a play area for the bird. This is usually preferred by owners who are not very tall, so cannot access the bird from the top of the cage. It is easier to access and of course, easier to clean. When you buy solid top cages, make sure that you get one that is rectangular or square in shape. The rounded ones do not allow free movement for the birds.

c) Where to place the cage?

The next challenge is finding a safe spot in your home to house the bird. When you choose a room to keep your bird cage in, make sure that:

- It is away from too much noise. Any room that faces the road or has loud traffic sounds is not a good idea, especially for a new bird. This room should not be the center of the family's activities either. A new bird will feel overwhelmed to see too many people and new faces. Even new voices can traumatize the bird.
- It does not have very bright and direct sunlight. While sunlight is necessary for the birds, if it gets too hot or direct, they may feel a little uneasy. You can even make a "dark spot" on the cage with a blanket to provide your bird with a hiding spot.
- There is a wall to place the cage against. This gives the bird a great sense of security. If the cage is right in the middle of the room, the bird may feel a little vulnerable and afraid.
- The bird is able to observe the family. While the bird should not be right in the middle of your daily activities, he or she should be able to observe the potential "flock". When the bird sees that you are happy in the space, it will also feel secure. Amazon parrots are very analytical birds and will learn a lot

from your body language, the food that you eat etc. Being able to observe you will make it easier for them to trust you eventually.

- Keep the cage away from the kitchen or AC vents. Smoke or toxins can be transmitted from these areas and can be fatal to your bird. For instance, Teflon fumes are toxic for birds and they should be protected from it.

d) Accessorize the cage

A bird cage does require some basic accessories besides the toys. The two most important ones are:

- **Food and water bowls:** Make sure that you get either steel or porcelain bowls for your birds. They should be shallow enough for your bird to reach out and eat or drink from them. If it seems like too much of a struggle, the bird may not eat or drink at all!

  Keep these bowls near the cage entrance. That way, it is easier for you to fill them up and clean them as well. You get special drinkers for birds that are almost like bottles for birds. This is not a necessity unless your vet advises you to do so for an ill bird. It is also important for you to keep a drinker for your bird if you see that it loves to splash around and make a mess. Amazon parrots love a good bath and will target their drinking bowl, even if you keep a separate bathing bowl for them.

- **The substrate:** We know now that birds poop a lot and there should be some substrate that can absorb this poop to keep the cage relatively clean. The best substrate to use for Amazon parrots is newspaper. It is cheaper, absorbs a lot better and is easier to clean out. Pine shavings or any wood shaving is not recommended, as it may be harmful for the bird. If you choose to use wood shavings, having a grate that separates the bird and the substrate is a good idea.

  Ideally, the substrate should be cleaned out every single day to avoid any dampness or chances of infections. In some pet stores, you may also be able to find special bird litter that can safely be used for your birds. If you do not like the idea of using newspaper, this is the best option for you.

Make all the housing preparations well in advance. You can even teach your family about the safe ways to approach the bird cage to avoid being bitten or hurt. The golden rule with Amazon parrots is to never overwhelm them. Making too much noise or suddenly approaching the bird when it is not expecting you to will startle it and make it react aggressively.

3) Quarantine preparations

If you already own other birds, quarantining the new bird is a necessity. When you bring home a new bird, you are introducing several spores, viruses and potential infections into the environment of your other birds. Even if the new bird looks perfectly healthy, chances are that it is a carrier of several diseases that can harm an entire flock. So, making proper quarantining arrangements is a must.

Quarantining is not a procedure that is restricted to people who want to breed or make a lucrative business with their bird. You have to do it even if you just have birds at home as pets. Many parrot owners may try to talk you out of this by saying that their new bird did not harm the flock in any way. In fact, they will also tell you that it is a nuisance that only makes the housebreaking process harder. You have to understand that quarantining is a preventive measure that is meant to keep your pet birds and also the rest of your family safe. You can contract several airborne diseases, too. So, you need to keep your birds quarantined for 30 days from the time they are introduced.

In an ideal situation, the bird that is quarantined should be kept away from the rest of the birds and stay fully isolated. It is a good idea to actually keep the bird in a completely different air space such as an outhouse or another room to protect the rest of the birds. If that is not possible, you definitely need to get a separate cage that you can quarantine the new bird in.

In homes that have forced air heating systems, the circulation leading to and from the room that the bird has been kept in should be cut off. Instead, opt for circulating the air from outside into this room for the best results. That way any spores in the air will also be removed effectively. The vents can lead to the circulation of disease-causing bacteria or fungi around the house.

For those who live in smaller apartments, you will have to just make sure that you find the furthest spot from your current flock to quarantine the bird. In addition to that, you must have the bird thoroughly checked by an avian vet to make sure that it is safe to have the new bird in your home. In most cases, this test will be done even before you actually bring the bird to your home.

The period of quarantine should be enough to ensure that the incubation period of any possible disease is complete before you introduce the bird to your flock. This is why a minimum of 30 days is recommended. However, it is a good idea to extend this period to six weeks if possible, as the incubation period of certain diseases could be this long. Once the incubation period is over, any existing disease will begin to show symptoms and you will be able to get necessary assistance for your birds.

Here are some tips to make sure that your quarantining measures are completely effective:

- Whenever you feed the birds, make sure that you feed your existing flock first and then move on to the quarantined bird. That way, you can prevent any chances of transmitting these diseases through dirty hands, clothing etc.
- In the room that you keep your quarantined bird in, keep an extra pair of clean clothes or atleast a smock and a pair of shoes. Whenever you approach the bird that needs to be quarantined, you will have to change from your regular clothes to these items of clothing. That way, you prevent any chances of getting bacteria or microbes on to the articles of clothing or on your shoes. These clothing items should be washed immediately after you have handled the bird.

- Before you get on with the rest of your routine, make sure that you take a quick shower. That will ensure that your birds are fully safe.

This may seem like quite a stretch initially. But, making it a full-time routine will keep your birds safe and will prevent the huge investments that you may have to make in case of any disease outbreak in your flock.

Now, if your bird has been rescued or adopted, your avian vet may even recommend that you provide your bird with some medication during this period of quarantining. Make sure that you have the stock of medication ready before you actually introduce the bird into your home. There are other exclusive cases like birds that have been kept in outdoor aviaries when the care you provide becomes more extensive. You may have to get your birds treated for conditions like giardia, coccidian and other soil-borne pathogens that may damage the entire flock .

In many cases, there are chances that your existing flock has had a latent disease within the birds. This may not have manifested or shown any symptoms. However, if you do introduce a new species, especially an exotic one like the Amazon parrot, there could be a sudden outbreak of the condition within the flock. Of course, every bird owner knows how hard it can be to take care of an entire flock that is suffering from a certain condition.

Make quarantining a priority for your birds and then you can introduce them to one another on neutral grounds.

What to do after the quarantine period finishes?

The first thing to do after your bird has completed the quarantine period is to bring him or her, in a different cage, into the room that houses your existing flock. This will help you check whether the flock or the new bird shows any signs of aggression or irritation. It is always wrong to assume that two birds will be friendly even if they belong to opposite genders in the same species of birds.

In homes where there are multiple birds, you have to introduce each bird to the new bird separately. Just let them live near one another in separate cages for a few days to see if there is any abnormal behavior in either birds. If your existing pet were to contract any disease from the new bird, you will be able to take care of a single bird quite easily.

Many people may tell you off for being over cautious with your birds. However, the disasters that can occur when you simply introduce the new bird to the flock are really not worth it. Making an extra effort for just 30 days can make sure that your entire flock is healthier and happier.

4) Parrot proofing the house

This is one of the most important parts of the preparation for a new bird. Before you bring your bird home, you need to make sure that the environment is safe for your bird. Here are some parrot proofing tips for you:

- The house should be 100% smoke free. In fact, many people recommend that homes with people who smoke should not have birds, as they can develop several respiratory issues.

- Keep the cage away from hard floors or concrete. If you clip the wings of your birds, you have to make sure that the bird will not fall and injure itself.

- Ceiling fans and table fans should be switched off when the bird is out. This is true even when your bird's wings are clipped. Even with wing clipping, a portion of the bird's flying ability is retained. As a result, the feathers or wings may get damaged.

- Get covers for all your stove tops or install a door in the kitchen. The kitchen should be a "no access" spot for birds because of the potential dangers in this area. Hot stoves, knives, fumes etc. can be extremely harmful for your birds.

- Cover up all the loose wires and threads. Parrots, being the inquisitive creatures they are, will tug at this and may end up injuring or electrocuting themselves.

- Make sure that doors and windows are closed whenever the bird is out of the cage. If you have a self-closing mechanism for your doors, have them removed and install strong stoppers. You do not want any flight-related mishaps due to slamming doors.

- Remove all plants that are harmful for birds. You can consult your vet or check online to make sure that none of the plants that you have are hazardous to your pet.

Parrot proofing is a must. Although you cannot be 100% safe at all times, taking the necessary measures to prevent any accidents is a must. Just keep an eye on your bird when it is out of the cage to be sure.

Chapter 4: The First Few Days

Parrots are highly intelligent creatures. They will analyze every situation and can even be highly emotional. This characteristic of these birds makes it hard for you to make changes easy on the birds. Simple things like going out in a car for the first time, a new human voice or a new face can be extremely traumatizing for these creatures. So, you can only imagine how hard the transition from a breeder, a pet store or a rescue home to your home can be for the bird. If you are unable to make this transition pleasant, that your bird may develop severe behavioral issues like aggression.

1) The first day of the parrot in your home

The time a bird takes to get used to a new home depends upon the bird's personality and its upbringing. Now, if your bird has been hand tamed, your interaction will be different and maybe, easier. However, for a bird that is not used to being handled, it will take longer for you to establish a relationship with the bird.

In any case, avoid over-handling the bird on the first day. When you bring them home, they are already stressed by the drive. So, the first thing you will do is let the bird into its enclosure. Just keep the bird's current cage's opening facing the opening of the enclosure and hold it there until your bird enters the new area.

Make plenty of food and water available to the bird. You need to feed the bird whatever it has been eating at the pet store or the breeder. Any change in diet should be made extremely gradually.

Then leave the bird in the cage. Do not talk to the bird or make excited noises or sounds. If you have several members in your family, ask them to keep away from the cage, at least for the first day. It is really tempting to handle the bird and play with it. But, on the first day, avoid it.

The most you can do is sit near the cage so that your bird is facing you eye to eye. Then place your hands on the sides of the cage and see if the bird approaches you. It may walk up, nibble or lick your fingers. Hold them steady and do not make any noise.

The first night is probably the hardest on the bird. Give it a sleeping space in the form of a readymade sleeping tent or even a blanket that it can hide behind. This makes sure that the bird gets enough recluse from the foreign sounds and sights in the new home.

2) The first few weeks

The first week is one of the most important bonding periods with your bird. Do not rush your bird to meet friends and family yet. You have 20 odd years to do that with your bird! Take this time to make your bird feel secure in your presence. Ensure that every interaction with your bird in this time is positive and enriching for the bird. You do not want to make your bird feel overwhelmed.

This is the time when you unleash the curiosity in your Amazon parrot. If your bird cage is small enough, pick it up and walk around the house and in a very soft voice tell him/her where he/she is. You can wait for a day or two if you have to transfer your bird into a travel cage to take it around. Let it feel the ambience of your home and start to feel like it is a part of it too.

If your bird is young, you need to make more time for it. You see, you are not just a companion but also a parent that this bird will actually learn from. You will train the bird, teach him/her to become more independent and even cuddle a little from time to time. Now, how the experiences of a bird turns out in your home depends entirely on the kind of attention that you give him/her. There are three *kinds* of attention that you need to give your bird:

- Focused attention: This means that all the time you spend with your bird is with complete attention to your bird. It is a one on one session with no distractions. There will be no television, other people from the household or even your mobile phone. This session is meant to educate your bird and train it instead of just playing.

- Ambient attention: This is when you and your bird are hanging out. You could be playing with new toys, using treats to get the bird to move around the cage etc. This is when you teach the bird to entertain itself even when you are in the room. This is when you lightly pet or stroke the bird occasionally while you continue with your routine such as reading or watching television.

- Casual attention: This is similar to ambient attention but you are a little more involved. Allow your bird to play with new toys and explore them. You will also engage in this activity and constantly encourage the bird. This is very necessary for you to develop a good bond with your bird and even keep him/her relatively independent.

For the first few weeks, you need to make sure that your bird gets an equal proportion of each type of attention. If one is more than the other, it affects the behavior of the bird. For example, if you give it too much focused attention, it will never learn to entertain itself. Instead, it will start screeching or even plucking its feathers when you are not in the same room.

It is advised that you restrict this attention to about 20 minutes every day. Once you start training your bird, make sure you establish a routine and stick to it. Preferably, this routine needs to be established from day 1. You need to fix a time to feed the bird, interact with it, train t etc. Parrots work really well with routines.

3) The first month

This is the best time to monitor the progress of your bird. They will get comfortable in this time and will begin to stick to your routine. If you have brought home a baby bird, they will grow up quite a bit in this period.

One thing you need to know with Amazon parrots is that they are slightly rebellious. They love to challenge authority from time to time just to see how far they can get. Especially with the juveniles, you can expect them to try to push the rule and routine that you have set for them. They may try biting or nipping and other such behavior. This is when you need to be extremely firm and tell them that you are boss.

Some parrot owners will recommend that you have the height of dominance with your bird. This means that you will never keep your eye level below the eye level of the bird but will always keep it above it. That is never a good idea because your bird may not interact comfortably with you because they will begin to see you as a threat. Instead, you should always stay at your bird's eye level so that it understands that you are a friend or an equal who means no harm. This is the best way to establish trust with your bird.

Here are a few rules that you must follow for the first month of your bird's time in your home:

- The diet should not be changed for at least a month from the time you bring the bird home. Any change will be made gradually by adding small proportions of the food that you want to give your bird with the food that it is already used to eating.

48

- Rules should be consistent. While you are trying to discipline your bird, being disciplined yourself is very important. If you slack, your bird will know that you are not firm enough and may not adhere to rules set by you.

- Do not have too many people over in this time. For the first month, avoid parties as much as you can. It will only make it harder for the bird to get used to its new home.

- Find a time when you are relatively free at work to bring the bird home. If you know that a certain month is demanding at your workplace and requires you to travel or spend long hours at the office, put your plans to bring a bird home on hold. This is a time when you cannot make any compromises on the time you spend with the bird.

4) Pets and children in your home

In the previous chapter we mentioned that some rescue shelters will not allow you to take a bird home if you have pets or children at home. This is done to protect your bird and the pets and children in your home.

With pets like cats and dogs, you must always remember that the bird is the weaker animal simply because of its smaller size. Even a playful nibble from a dog will be fatal for a bird. These creatures play the role of prey animals in the wild and are always under threat.

If you have a cat or dog at home that you want your bird to interact with, start with caged interactions. The bird is in the cage while your pet cat or dog will explore. This is when your cat or dog may try to get in the cage. Make sure that you prohibit this behavior right in the beginning. When your cat or dog is so used to the bird's presence that they do not really care too much about it, you can let the bird out of the cage. Remember to supervise this interaction at all times, even if your cat or dog is very friendly and gentle.

The idea is to never challenge the instincts of your pets. Of course, birds and pets can be great friends. But, it is best not to take that chance unless they have grown up together. If you introduce them to one another as babies, the equation is very different. In any case, the saliva of the pet, particularly a cat is toxic for a bird. So, do not let the bird out of the cage if you are not around.

When it comes to children, the excitement that the children will have towards the new pet is the biggest challenge. If the bird is startled or caught off guard, chances are that it will attack.

In addition to that, children may be naughty at times and may playfully tease the bird. This does not go down well with the Amazon parrot and they will bite or attack. It is common for a child to scream when this happens. Now, mostly, biting is an act of communication as opposed to aggression. When the child calls out in fear, the bird gets a fitting response and will believe that this is a great way to get attention.

If you have children at home who are under 12 years of age, make sure that you supervise all the interactions. Tell the children that they need to be very careful while interacting with birds. Teach them compassion towards their new pets. Discourage any behavior that can scare the parrot. You see, birds do not understand that they are children. If the child is a threat to the bird, it will believe that all humans are a threat and will begin to behave rather badly around them.

A new bird takes a lot of patience from the owner. If you are able to make this period delightful for the bird, you will have a friend for life. They will always love you and will, of course, be extremely entertaining.

For owners who have kids after the bird arrives

Now this is an entirely different story. You may have a baby after the bird has been in your house. If your bird is well trained by then and has formed a strong bond with one of the family members, this is harder than you think.

When the baby arrives, the important thing to do would be to make sure that your bird is getting as much attention as the child. This should be done by keeping your bird around whenever you are playing with the baby, changing or feeding the baby etc. If you have a habit of going to the bird only when the baby is asleep or away, the baby becomes a threat to the bird. The bird begins to understand that when the baby is around, it will not get love. This may even make it aggressive towards the baby.

Chapter 5: Bonding with Amazon Parrots

With parrots, the term bonding has a lot more meaning than just being the person who plays with the bird and feeds it. Now, bonding with parrots means that you will have to share your experiences and interests with the bird. To a parrot, you could even be it mate or companion. Now, with Amazon parrots, you can expect to form a very strong bond if you are willing to be patient and calm from day 1.

These birds tend to bond more with one person in the household. They will be cordial to the other family members. But the human that they bond with holds a very special place in their lives. If you want to be that person, then you have to start spending a lot of your time gaining your bird's trust. Unless you are able to make the bird feel secure in your presence, it is not possible to establish a strong bond.

1) Building Trust with Step Up training

As mentioned before, building trust is the first step to forming a bond. Now, stepping up is the ultimate display of trust from a bird towards its owner. This process can take a few months or even just a few hours. It really depends upon the personality of the bird that you have in your home.

Start by getting the bird out of the cage. Remember not to force the bird out of the cage. If you try to hold him/her and get him/her out of the cage or just nudge him/her with a target or treat, it may get the bird out of the cage but it will do nothing to strengthen the bond. The bird will learn that you do not respect its wishes to stay inside the cage.

Target training is one of the best ways to get the bird out of the cage. First put a treat on the end of a small stick and extend it to the bird. The bird will either accept the treat or will ignore it. Once the bird accepts the treat, repeat this a few times until the bird understands that the stick equals a treat. The stick becomes the target.

Now try to move the target around and see if the bird follows it. Most likely, your parrot will follow the stick because it expects a treat. Then, open the cage and place the target just at the entrance. As the bird approaches the target, draw it back until your bird is finally out of the cage.

Then, just let it explore the space. It may climb up the cage, walk around it or just look around. Make sure that there are no pets or other disturbing objects around the bird. Even the smallest negative experience will make it a lot harder for you to establish trust with your bird. After a few minutes outside the cage, place a treat or toy inside the cage and lead the bird back in. Placing a treat is necessary to tell your bird that the cage is a fun place to go back to.

Now, it is time to start step up training. Open the cage door and place your finger horizontally like a perch. Then, keep the target right behind the finger and say "step up". If the bird bites your finger, do not panic. It is only making sure that the perch is steady. If the bite scares you, you can even use a wooden perch. But, remember not to suddenly draw your finger away. The bird will believe that it is an unsteady perch and will lose trust.

If the bird steps up, praise it and give it a treat. If he/she does not step up, don't force it too much. Let your bird take its time to gain trust. The moment your bird steps up, keep the finger steady for several minutes and put the bird back in the cage.

The next step is to try the step up command without the target. Your voice cue will be enough now. The moment you say "Step Up", your bird will step on to your finger.

You may use the same technique to get the bird to step up on your shoulder and also on your head. This is the ultimate test of trust for your bird. There will come a time when stepping down or going back into the cage will become undesirable to your feathered pal. That is why you need to add toys and treats into the cage everytime you put him/her back. You see, separation is a negative emotion for birds. They will resist it unless they know that separation leads to something more fun.

Step up training is very important for birds. In case of a fire, or a natural calamity, having a bird who is trained to step up is easier to rescue. Even if your bird gets into an ugly situation with family pets, you can just ask him/her to step up on your finger and get him/her out of the unpleasant situation.

After the step up training, you are ready to take your bird along for all your chores and make it a part of your routine. Of course, the more time you spend with him/her, the stronger your bond will get.

2) Keeping your bird entertained

Once your Amazon parrot begins to trust you, you can begin to play with the bird and have some meaningful interactions with the bird. The more you find ways to entertain your bird, the better he/she will be health-wise. There are several things that you can do to give your bird the mental and physical stimulation he/she needs.

Toys

Get your parrot several toys that he/she can play with. There are four types of toys that you must get your bird:

Chewable toys

When you put a chewable toy in your bird's cage, know that it will be torn apart in minutes. These toys are a lot of fun for birds and actually gives them a feeling of accomplishment for ripping the toy apart. This activity is very good for the bird's beak as well. It will keep the bird active and in a playful mood all the time after playing with these toys. Some of these toys are made from pine and soft wood, plastic, leather, cotton rope and even paper. You will also get a few chew toys that have mineral supplements in them to help your bird.

Foraging toys

All birds love to forage. These toys mimic the food gathering activity of birds in the wild. Hide the food in them and make your bird look for the food. In the process, the bird's mind is fully engaged while they try to figure out a way to get the food out. There are different varieties of foraging toys. Some of them are made from plastic or other material that cannot be destroyed. Others are meant for the bird to just tear apart. You can even make foraging toys at home by bundling up a few treats in a newspaper and giving it to the bird.

The only problem with the permanent toys is that your bird may just figure out how it works. After that he/she will simply be bored with the toy and may not even play with it! The newspaper idea works best and is a favorite amongst birds. Just add a few more layers of paper to make the difficulty level higher.

Physical activity toy

There are some toys that make sure that your bird's muscles are engaged while he/she uses them. Swings and perches are the best examples of physical activity toys. Your bird will also enjoy this because this mimics their natural habitat, which includes vines and branches that they like to play with. Besides this, there are several other things like ladders that you can install in the cage.

Just make sure that you do not overcrowd the cage with toys for the bird. The cage should be large enough for the bird and all the toys that the bird will need for recreation. Keep recycling the toys regularly. If you find something that is covered in feces or dirt, take it out immediately, as it is a place for bacteria and fungi to thrive.

Spend time outdoors

Taking your bird outdoors is a great way to bond with it. However, your outdoor adventures should be carefully planned to make sure that your bird does not get startled and escape or get injured. Going outdoors is also a good idea for the bird's health, as they will require a least 15 minutes of direct sunlight every week. However, you need to make sure that it is not too hot or cold when you take your bird out.

If your bird is not hand-tamed or does not know how to step up, it is not safe to let the bird out of the cage or carrier even with a harness. In case your bird gets into a messy situation, you can pick the bird up and get it away if it is hand tamed.

For the first few days, take the bird out in a carrier and let it get used to the surroundings. The bird needs to look around and soak in the new sounds and sights. Let the bird get comfortable with these new situations and visions. You will know by the bird's body language. If the bird is afraid, he/she will retreat to a corner. Head tilting and jittery body language suggests that the bird is too afraid of the new environment. But, when the bird is comfortable, he/she will approach the wall of the cage and even interact with you quite normally.

You can use a parrot harness and take the bird out of the carrier. Make sure that you hold on to this leash to prevent any escapes if your bird just gets scared or startled by a new experience outdoors. At the same time, do not yank at the leash as you may end up injuring the bird.

When you take your bird out, you need to be extremely watchful. If you see any threat such as a neighbor's cat, put your bird back in the carrier. The outdoors also provides a great neutral ground for you to train your bird.

Birds that are taken outdoors more often are more socialized. They will take a look at new people, new faces, animals and other visuals. Chances are people will approach the cage. Encourage this under your supervision to make your bird more socialized.

When you regularly take your bird out, it becomes much easier for you to take your bird to the vet, to a groomer or even to generally travel with your bird. A bird who is more social is also easier to care for when you are away. They will be comfortable with other people taking care of them in your absence, too.

That said, make sure that your bird is safe from insect bites or mosquito bites. That can lead to unwanted diseases and infections in your beloved bird. You can ask your vet how to keep your bird safe from these bites.

3) The talkative Amazon parrot

Amazon parrots are among the most talkative parrots on the planet. They love to observe their human family and mimic the sounds that they make. It is possible to train the birds to say things that you want them to. However, they will also pick up other words that they will hear around the house.

An amazon parrot picks up language just as a child would. The more time you spend talking to the bird, the more words he/she will learn. The thing with Amazon parrots is that they are highly intelligent birds that can also understand the context that certain words are being said in.

It is necessary to form a routine to train your bird to speak as well. Consistency is the key if you want to teach your bird specific words and phrases.

Pick a time in the day when your bird has eaten and is in a good mood. Take away all the distractions like toys and sit with your bird. Repeat whatever you want the bird to learn in a high pitched, excited voice. Keep doing this every day until the bird learns them.

You will notice the bird mumble to itself all day long. This is him/her practicing to say the words that you are trying so hard to teach them. Eventually, the bird will speak out the words that you have been teaching it. With Amazon parrots, you can even teach them full songs.

To initiate the birds into speaking, you can even run DVDs that are available at pet stores. You can even let your bird watch cartoons or television for some time every day. The shows that have loud and high pitched voices work the best for birds.

Make sure that you keep talking to the bird whenever you feed it or approach the cage. However, be careful about what you say around your bird. You definitely do not want your bird to say something embarrassing when you are trying to host a classy dinner for your friends and family.

4) Body language

The most important part of bonding with your parrot is understanding what he/she is trying to communicate with you. Vocalization is very common among Amazon parrots. However, they also use their body extensively to communicate. Understanding this language will help you know the mood of your bird. But, more importantly, you will know if your bird is feeling sick. Here are a few tips to read your bird's body language:

Flapping the wings: This is a bird's way of telling you that he/she needs more attention from you.

Fluffing of the feather: Feather fluffing is the bird's way of releasing their tension. However, if the feather remains fluffed for a long period of time, it is a sign that the bird is not feeling too good.

The dance: A parrot who wants your attention or wants you to give him/her something will do an attention-seeking dance. It will sit just at the entrance of the cage and will keep moving its head back and forth.

Keeping the head down: This is another sign for you to approach and pet the bird. When a bird does this, it is telling you that it wants you to pet him/her.

The aggressive stance: There are certain experiences that are unpleasant for a bird. They may not be in the mood for play or might be feeling threatened by something in their environment. That is when they will assume the aggressive stance. There are several displays of aggression as far as Amazon parrots are concerned. They may fan the tail and sway with the chest held up, hissing, spitting, dilating the pupils and keeping the body low with the mouth open is a sign of aggression in birds.

Stretching: Just like us humans, birds love to stretch too. This lets them lubricate all their joints and just relax their muscles completely. When parrots stretch, they often display mantling, which is stretching one leg and wing at the same time.

Bobbing: Bobbing the head or the tail is a way the parrot seeks attention. This behavior can become rather neurotic in birds that have been caged for a long time. You have to also watch the energy levels of the bird. If bobbing occurs despite low energy, it is a sign of illness.

Quivering wings: The bird will rapidly shake its wings to show excitement. In some cases, it may also be a sign of fear in the bird. When they are in the breeding season, this quivering is a sort of dance that is performed for the mate.

Beak positions: If the beak is open while the body is crouched, this is a sign of fear in birds. This is the bird warning you that he/she will bite if you get too close. This may also be accompanied by hissing and screeching in your bird.

Language of poop: This is the body language displayed by birds when they are just about to poop. You need to learn this to potty train your bird. The bird will back up and crouch while lifting its tail. The moment it does this, you can shift the bird to another place where you would like it to poop.

Scratching: Also known as chicken scratching, this is a playful behavior displayed by birds. In the process, they may end up making a mess in your home or in the cage.

Pinning the eye: Pinning means to rapidly dilate and contract the pupils. This behavior is displayed by birds either when they are very excited or when they are angry.

Drooping the wing: In some species, this is a part of the mating dance. However, in most cases wings that are drooping indicate illness in the bird.

Wing flipping: This is common behavior shown by birds that are irritated. The bird may even be trying to get your attention. In some cases, wing flipping is seen in birds that are about to enter the molting season.

Lying down on the back: This is playful behavior in most parrots. However, check the breathing and the movement in the bird's body when you notice this.

When you are trying to study your bird's body language, also keep an eye on the surroundings of the bird. Since they usually have two emotions associated with one type of behavior, the immediate environment will help you decide what your bird is actually trying to communicate with you. As you spend more time with your bird, you will also learn body language specific to your pet.

Chapter 6: Caring for your Amazon Parrot

As a responsible bird parent, you need to make sure that your parrot gets the best care possible. This chapter talks about various elements of a good care routine that you need to develop for your bird.

1) Feeding your bird

Good nutrition is the most important part of parrot care. You need to make sure that your bird gets a balanced meal that will provide it with all the nutrients required.

In most cases, breeders will keep birds on an all seed diet. This can be harmful for your bird, as it is a high source of fats and a very low source of vital nutrients. However, you will not change this diet for at least one month from the time the bird arrives in your home. Give it some time to settle in before you make any changes.

When you do begin to change the diet, don't do it drastically. Slowly include the food that you want it to eat. Then, you can decrease the proportion of the undesirable foods in the diet. Here are the crucial things that you must include in your bird's diet:

- Pellets: Dry bird pellets are available in any pet supply store. This forms a major part of your bird's diet. It is a good idea to ask your vet to suggest something that will work well for your bird.

- Fresh fruits and vegetables: Except avocado and lettuce, you can give your Amazon parrot most fruits and vegetables. These are the primary sources of vitamins and minerals that are essential for the well-being of the bird. Try a variety of fresh fruits and vegetables. Your bird will pick its favorites. It is a good idea to heat the produce up a little before you give it to your bird.

- Nuts and seeds: These food items should only be used as treats. They are very useful in training your bird. However, if you give your bird these foods on a regular basis, they will not really be excited by it.

Every morning, clean out the food and water bowls and refill them. Even if it means that you have to throw away the left overs, do so. Then at about noon, you can give your bird fruits and vegetables. Treats should be restricted to training and disciplining drills. Make sure that your bird has enough fresh water available as well. If your bird needs it, your vet will prescribe supplements that you may include in the diet of your bird as per the instructions of your vet.

2) Grooming the bird

Grooming is not a daily routine with birds because they spend most of their time preening themselves. However, in order to keep any debris or dirt away from the bird's body, bathing the bird once every 15 days is a good idea. Grooming activities also include wing clipping and trimming of the toes and the beak. But it takes a lot of care to carry out these grooming activities in order to ensure that the bird is not hurt in the process.

Bathing

Bathing the bird does not require too much effort. If you do not notice any debris or dirt that has matted down the feathers, it is not even necessary to use soap. Just misting the body of the bird with water is good enough.

When you are misting your bird's body, you will never spray water on its face or eyes directly. In addition, watch the bird's body language very carefully. If you feel like the bird is retreating or backing away, do not continue to mist the body. This clearly shows that it is not enjoying it. On the other hand, a bird that is enjoying the bath will lift its wings and turn around while you mist its body.

You can also bathe your bird with a shallow water bath. If you want to draw the bird to this bath, just add a few pieces of spinach into the container. The bird will step in and splash around while it forages through the food. This is one of the simplest and most stress-free methods to get the bird into a bath.

If you notice any matting or debris on the bird's feathers, you can clean it using a wash cloth and some mild soap. Make sure that the soap is washed out of the bird's body completely. Birds will continue to preen themselves. Any chemicals from the soap on the body of the bird can be ingested, leading to poisoning.

After the bird is bathed, make sure that it does not get too close to the air-conditioning. Some parrot owners may advise using a hair dryer after a bath. However, this is not necessary, as the birds will preen their wet feathers into place.

Wing clipping

Some bird owners will do this at home themselves. However, you may get the blood feather accidentally while clipping the primary feathers. It is a simple service that costs about $15 or £8. You need to get the wing clipped just once every 6 months. So, it is best that you get it done by an expert.

You could even do this at home if you have some experience or training with it. Wrap the bird in a towel and place the bird on your lap. From the loose end, extend one wing and clip about 1 cm of the three longest feathers or the primary feathers. Repeat the same on the other side. Then, open both the wings out to make sure that they are equal.

If the wings of the bird are not equally clipped, the balance of the bird will be compromised. It will not even be able to balance on the perch. So, unless you are completely sure, do not clip the wings of your bird at home.

In case you do get a blood feather in the process and it bleeds, make sure that you apply flour immediately. Using a styptic pencil also works well to control bleeding of the blood feathers.

Toe nail and beak trimming

The toe nails and beak of your Amazon parrot will get really sharp. This is not ideal, as the fibre used in our upholstery will end up getting caught in the sharp ends. If the bird moves suddenly when its toe or beak is caught, it can cause serious injuries.

In addition, birds tend to nip and bite playfully. If the beak is too sharp, you may even hurt yourself. So, it is a good idea to trim the toe nails and beak.

Just place a finger under the sharp end of the beak or toe. Using a nail file, gently file the sharp end. Keep feeling the end. When it begins to feel rounded and blunt you must stop. You must not trim the beak and toes too much, as they are used by the bird to climb and handle their food.

Trim the beak and toe whenever you feel like it has become too sharp and has begun to get caught in fabric or other surfaces of your home.

Grooming your bird regularly instills a lot of trust. The more time you spend grooming your bird, the closer it will get to you. It also makes you comfortable with handling your bird and taking good care of it.

3) Cleaning the cage

Keeping your bird's cage clean is one of the most important routines. If the cage is poorly managed or badly maintained, your bird may develop several health issues realted to hygiene and sanitation. You see, birds tend to poop and actually make quite a mess that you need to keep cleaning. These damp and dirty areas become breeding grounds for certain microbes that can be deadly for your bird! There is a routine that you need to follow when you clean your bird's cage. Only when you maintain this routine will you be able to keep your bird's environment free from any possible health hazards.

Daily routine:

There are a few areas in the cage that you must clean on a daily basis for perfect hygiene.

The lining that you use or the substrate needs to be changed on a daily basis, there is no doubt in that. Using a substrate like newspaper is good as it is highly absorbent in nature. Amazon parrots are medium-sized birds, which means that you will only need a few layers of this substrate. The best time to change the substrate everyday is when you are feeding your birds in the morning. Take the food and water bowls out and change the substrate as well.

The food and water bowls must be emptied out fully every morning. Even if there are pellets left out in the food bowl, it needs to be cleaned out. When you are giving your birds fruits and vegetables, the remaining food should not be allowed to sit idle for more than an hour. It should be removed immediately. Eventually you will know how much your bird can actually eat and you can avoid wastage.

Now, when you wash the dishes, you can do so with mild soap solution. Make sure it is extremely diluted. If your vet has recommended any disinfectant, you can use it to clean the bowls too. Wash the soap out thoroughly. There should be no traces of it whatsoever.

Lastly, you need to make sure that the dishes are fully dry before you replace them in the cage. It is actually a great idea to have two sets of bowls so that you can clean one and replace the other. That way, there is no chance of any dampness.

If you are using a water botte for the cage, you will need to use a proper bottlebrush and clean it out on a dail basis. Another cage accessory that needs to be cleaned everyday is the birdbath. Disinfect it thoroughly, refill the water and then place it back.

The area around your cage needs to be cleaned up everyday. Make sure that you vacuum out any seeds, feathers or debris near the cage. This is very important when you have other pets or multiple birds in your household. Of course, with kids in the house, you will have to be additionally careful.

Weekly or Monthly cleaning

There needs to be a thorough clean up every week or month to get the cage cleaned out inside and out. For medium-sized birds like the Amazon Parrot, monthly cleaning is recommeneded. However, if your bird is unwell or if you have received special instructions from your vet, you can do the same every week. Your weekly or monthly cleaning routine consists of seven steps:

- Get all your cleaning supplies in place. You do not want to scramble around for them. You can make a cleaning kit for your bird that consists of paper towels, cage wipes, substrate material, cleaning cloth, recommended disinfectant, a scrub brush or even a toothbrush and sandpaper. You will need a garbage bag to pack all the debris and dirt up.

- The bird should be removed from the cage and placed in a transfer cage. You may use the cage that you normally use when you take your bird to the vet. You need to ensure that it is not accidentally exposed to any fumes while making this transfer.

- Take all the toys and accessories out of the cage.

- Any loose dropping should be removed from inside the cage. Scrub the bars and the floor with warm and diluted soap water. You can even put the cage in a tub or place it under the shower. Then after you have scrubbed and rinsed it throuroughly, you will spray it with a disinfectant recommended by your vet and rinse it again. Make sure you air dry the cage. Keeping it out in the sun will destroy most microorganisms.

- Droppings should be removed from the toys and the perches using soap water. Using sandpaper makes this easier for you.

Just as you did with the cage, wash the toys and all the accessories first before you spray them with the disinfectant and wash them thoroughly again. The toys, accessories and perches must be sun dried before you put them back. In some cases, if the quality and material of the toy or accessory allows it, you can even dry them in the oven at a temperature of 250 degrees. It will take only 15 minutes for it to dry thoroughly.

- Clean up the area around the cage and under it. Make sure you take a look at the walls for any cobwebs or dust particles, too.

- Put all the accessories back into the cage. Lay the substrate, fill the food and water bowl and bring the bird back into the clean and shiny cage.

Tips on choosing the right cleaning agent:
There are a few natural cleaning agents that you can use to keep your bird's cage clean. Here are some of the safest and most recommended options for you:

- You can use a very mild soap that has been diluted well. It is one of the best options to get the toys and the perches cleaned.

- A solution of distilled vinegar and water is also a good idea, as it cleans the cage thoroughly. You need to make a solution with about 1 cup of vinegar per gallon of water.

- You can even use steam to get to the nooks and crannies of your toys or the cage. You must only use clean water in the steamer in order to get the best possible results. No other liquid is safe for use either.

- Grapefruit seed extract is an unusual but highly effective choice for cleaning the cage. Now, traditionally this is used to clean any surface like the kitchen counter, cutting board or any other place that has had some food kept on it for a while.

- Baking soda is a great ingredient to remove any oil or grease. When used as a paste, mixed with water, you can also use it to remove any stains on the surface.

Following this routine also allows you to check for:
- Any change in the amount of food that your bird is eating.
- Regurgitated material in or around the cage.
- Abnormal droppings thst are strange in quantity or even color.
-Fraying of suspended toys, which would have to be replaced immediately.
- The condition of the cage in general.

When you develop a routine for cage cleaning, you can actually come across several early signs of illness or disease in your bird. Anything that is not normal should be reported to your vet immediately so that your bird can get timely attention. Of course, cage cleaning is also a wonderful bonding activity for the bird and its owner.

4) Travelling with the bird
Travelling with your Amazon parrot is a process. If you are taking your bird out in the car, you need to ensure that the bird is used to this new environment.

The first thing to do would be to keep the bird in the car for a few minutes and observe its reaction. If he/she is calm and composed, you can try to drive around the block. If he/she gets edgy and scared, take him/her back inside.

When driving in the car with your bird, you need to ensure that the temperature is maintained at room temperature. Place the cage in a place where there are no drafts as you drive along. Of course, you need to add additional layers of substrate if you are going on a long drive. Birds will seldom "go" when they are in a moving vehicle. If you are going on a long drive with the bird, stopping every 20 minutes is recommended to help the bird recover and calm down.

Travelling overseas

Travelling overseas with your Amazon parrot requires a lot of preparation. The first thing is to find out about the laws involved with Amazon parrots in the country that you are travelling to. Then, you need to make sure that you find an airline that will take good care of your bird during the flight. They will need to be fed and given clean water. Very few airlines provide these services.

The laws of travelling

Normally, travelling within your country should not be a problem. In the United States of America, each state may have separate laws about having Amazon parrots or importing them. Checking with the Wildlife Authority of that state is a good idea before you take your bird along.

Sometimes, a certain species of bird can be banned because of quarantining issues. One classic example is the ban on parrots that was issued in the Southwestern region of the United States when Exotic New Castle's disease broke out. In these cases, you may not be allowed to cross the borders of a state with your parrot.

It is also recommended that you contact reputed vets in the area that you are travelling to in order to check for any possible restrictions. Some states require you to carry a health certificate with your bird. This can be provided by your avian vet. The certificate should not be older than 10 days prior to your date of travel. Even when you are driving, make sure you take care of all the legalities, as some states will have checks at the border.

It is a bigger challenge to travel with an exotic bird species. You have to take care of two things- all the export laws in your country and all the import laws in the country that you are heading to.

It is necessary for you to obtain a CITES permit to take a bird out of your state. This permit is an agreement of sorts that countries across the world have signed with respect to the import of various species into their country. The primary objective of this is to make sure that the birds are not traded illegally. You can log on to the

CITES website to check for the authority that issues this permit in your country. In the USA, it is issued by the Office of Management Authority of Fish and Wildlife Services.

This is a lengthy process and requires you to apply for the permit at least 20 days before you plan to travel. Once the permit is obtained, make several copies of it and carry it with you during your trip. You will also have to present a health certificate issued by a certified avian vet.

It is also necessary to check if the CITES permit is enough in the country that you are travelling to. While most countries require just this, some may have local laws governing the entry and exit of exotic birds in their country. They may require an export certificate or even specific medical check-ups to be completed before allowing your bird across the border.

The actual journey

You need to find an airline that will take care of your bird during a long flight. Some airlines will provide food and water to your bird at regular intervals at a small additional fee. Here are some tips to make sure that your bird is safe during the flight:

- Get a good quality carrier. Check with the airline if they have any specifications with respect to the carrier that you use for your bird.

- If you need to change flights, make sure you take the same airline during the transit. That way you are familiar with all the rules of the airline and will not have to make any changes along the way.

- Place water in a bottle drinker or a commercially available drinker. That way, the water will not spill and mess up the cage.

- Add several layers of substrate. This will not only prevent the cage from getting messy but will also ensure that it is well cushioned to keep the bird safe. Using a harness is recommended for a long flight.

- Place the bird's favorite toys in the cage to make sure that it does not feed too stressed.

- Clip the wings of your bird to make the customs process easier. In case the bird gets out of the cage or the carrier, it would be quite a nuisance to find a fully flighted bird in a strange airport.

- As soon as you arrive at the hotel or your new home, get the bird checked by an avian vet thoroughly.

Moving overseas when you have a parrot is something to think about. If you have to move for a job or any other reason, you need to pick a country where bringing an Amazon parrot is legal. If not, having to give your bird away can be the hardest thing to do.

If you are only travelling temporarily, it is a good idea to avoid the stress of travelling for your bird. Find a friend or relative who can take care of the bird in your absence. It is preferable that they stay in your home and take care of the bird. In case that is not an option, take your bird to your friend or relatives home a couple of times before you depart. This will familiarize your bird with the new environment and will make it less stressful.

Alternatively, you can hire a pet sitter from a reputed agency to take care of your bird. Make sure that the sitter has enough experience with your parrot species, has access to emergency care if required and has a substitute to take care of the bird in case he or she is unavailable. Leave your phone number as well as your vet's number if you are putting the bird into a pet sitter's care.

Some tips for owners who hire pet sitters
When you are looking for a reliable pet sitter to make sure that your parrot is well taken care of in your absence, you need to look

for someone who knows their stuff. Here are a few tips that you need to keep in mind when you are hiring a pet sitter:

- The sitter should be a recommended one. You can get one by the recommendation of other pet parents or you can look for a professional agency to hire your pet sitter from. The National Association of Professional Pet Sitters is one such organization that you can hire your sitter from.

- Before you hire the pet sitter, make sure that you interview him or her once. This will allow you to check out your rapport with the individual and also the genuine ability of this person to take care of your bird.

- Watch the interaction of your potential pet sitter with your parrot. Is the sitter comfortable handling your bird? If not, how will he or she be able to manage in your absence?

- Ask for the experience that the sitter has with these birds. Amazon parrots have different requirements when it comes to food and care. Is the sitter aware of this? In addition to that, you also need to be sure that your sitter is smart enough to learn fast enough.

- If the sitter is unable to make it to work some day, what are the arrangements that he or she will be making? Are there enough substitutes to take care of the bird in case the sitter is unavailable for several reasons.

- Does the sitter know basic first aid to be given to birds? If not, how is he or she equipped to deal with emergencies?

Once you have satisfactory answers to all these questions you should hire the pet sitter. It is best if the sitter is able to stay in your home to take care of your bird. Some of them may even prefer to keep the cage in their own homes and watch the bird. That can be quite a hassle, as the bird will get extremely stressed.

5) Care during the breeding season

Amazon parrots will attain sexual maturity by about 6 months of age. The primary breeding season for these birds is during spring. The moment your bird reaches sexual maturity, they will become hormonal and will want to find a mate for themselves.

While bonding is recommended, you must never let your parrot believe that you are his mate. Always restrict behavior like feeding from your mouth or your plate, stroking the neck of the bird and cuddling. If your parrot believes that you are his mate, it will get frustrated and irritable during this season. This will make your bird resort to behaviors like feather plucking. You will also notice sudden aggression towards members of your family, especially your children and spouse.

You will know that your bird is hormonal when:

- The bird crouches with trembling feathers.
- The bird regurgitates in front of you.
- The bird lifts the vent when cuddling with you, in the case of a female.
- The bird mounts your hand and grips your thumb, in the case of a male.
- There is a sudden increase in appetite.
- The bird flirts with you by performing a mating dance, bobbing the head or even flinging the wings around.
- The bird, particularly the female, becomes very territorial.
- The bird screams incessantly or attacks your family members.

This is when you have two options. You may either find your bird a mate or you may deter the breeding behavior in your bird. If you decide to find a mate, you need to introduce the birds with proper quarantining as mentioned before. The bird you introduce should be checked by a vet for the gender, as Amazon parrots are not sexually dimorphic. This means that the male and the female look alike.

Parrots bond for life. So, if you do plan on getting a mate for your bird, you need to be prepared to care for the hatchlings and the parents year after year.

Discouraging breeding behavior
The breeding season is very stressful for the birds as well as their owners. This is the time when you need to take additional care of the bird, deal with behavioral changes and even watch the eggs and hatchlings carefully. While this may appeal to some, it is quite a hassle to others. If you do not want your birds to breed or if you do not want to introduce a mate for your bird:

- Reduce the length of the day by putting the bird to sleep early. This can be done by putting a blanket on the cage or by keeping the cage in a room with little sunlight. This provides a false notion that it is still spring.

- The bird should be away from enclosed and dark spaces. Remove any small boxes or shadowy areas from the cage to prevent nesting behavior. Birds may look for spaces like under the bed or behind the curtain to fulfill their nesting needs. Keep an eye on the bird to prevent this.

- If your bird has closely bonded with the other birds in an aviary, keep it away from them. This well reduce the hormonal urges in your bird.

- Be very careful about letting your bird believe that you are the mate. As mentioned before, do not encourage certain behaviors in the bird.

- During the day, your bird must get full spectrum sunlight and also a good diet. When the calcium and mineral metabolism is sped up by the sunlight, your bird will stay healthy even if she lays unfertilized eggs. This happens in highly hormonal birds, making them weak due to nutrition depletion.

- If your birds are single, remove soft toys, mirrors and other toys that can substitute a mate. You will see the bird display aforementioned hormonal behaviors towards certain toys. Make sure that they are removed immediately.

• Change the interiors of the cage and also the location of the cage. This is especially important for the females, as they will be less territorial when they are in an unfamiliar space.

• If your bird has laid such an egg, do not remove it. Let the bird brood over these eggs. That discourages the need to lay more eggs.

• If the bird lays eggs excessively, you can speak to your vet to provide any injections to make her immune to these hormonal urges.

If you face any challenges while dealing with a hormonal bird, your vet is the best person to help you out. They will be able to provide medicines and also injections that make the birds less hormonal. The right kind of nutrition is also necessary to prevent this type of behavior. Your vet can help you with most of these requirements.

Caring for nesting birds
If you decide that you want to find a mate for your bird and encourage breeding, you need to make sure that you provide a conducive environment for this to be successful. The birds should be given proper nutrition to prevent laying soft eggs, damaged eggs and also the transmission of diseases to the eggs.

When the birds are in the breeding season and you have found a suitable mate for your pet, here are a few things that you need to do in order to prepare them to start mating:
• Shift the cage to a quiet and cozy room. The birds should not have any disturbance.

• It is a good idea to have a separate breeding cage to ensure that neither of the birds get too territorial.

- Place a nesting box outside this cage. You can use a shoe box or even purchase commercially-made nesting boxes for your bird.

- Increase the protein level in the diet of the birds. The female especially will need calcium supplementation to make sure that the eggs are healthy. You need to add mineral and calcium blocks in the cage as well. This will keep the bird well nourished.

- You may have to add artificial lighting in the room to increase the number of hours with light. The longer the day feels, the more likely the birds are to mate.

When the birds are ready to mate, the male will mount the female. After this mating ritual, it will take about 10 days for the bird to lay the first egg. Make sure that you do not disturb the birds too often. The only time you will interact with the bird is when you feed them or if the female develops complications like egg binding.

Following this, the female will lay one egg each day or maybe one every alternate day. The average clutch size is about 8-12 eggs.

The incubation period for Amazon parrot eggs is 18-23 days. Most often, the female will hatch the eggs and care for the hatchlings with the help of the male. However, in some cases, they may simply abandon the eggs.

In case the eggs are abandoned, you will have to set up an incubator to hatch them. Most incubators will come with instructions to set up the heat and the light in such a way that they resemble the natural warmth of the female's body.

Caring for the hatchlings

There are various options when it comes to raising the chicks. You may allow the parents to raise the chicks all by themselves.

In this case, the birds are not hand tamed and may be less social. This is why most breeders prefer to hand tame the chicks.

If the parent birds are caring for the hatchlings you need to keep an eye on how the parents are behaving towards them. Sometimes, one of the parents is aggressive towards the chicks and may even kill a few. That is when you will intervene and take the birds into your care.

Hatchlings raised by parents will continue to stay in the nest box with the parents and will be fed by them. In four weeks they will fledge completely. In this time, if the female is preparing to lay another clutch, she will turn hostile towards the chicks. This is yet another cue for you to take over the parenting role.

The best option is to let the birds be cared for by the parents for a few weeks before you remove them from the nest. Ideally, Amazon parrot chicks should be left in the nest for at least 10-12 days before you remove them and place them in a brooder. Readymade brooders are available. If you want to make one yourself, you can get a large enough cardboard box and provide infra-red heating lamps. The temperature should be set to 92 degrees Fahrenheit in order for the chicks to survive.

Hand-feeding the birds requires a small syringe that can pass the food on. The food is a specially-made chick formula that your vet can recommend. You get several commercially made formula that you may use as is. It is also a good idea to add mashed fruits like papaya to make the formula more nutritious for your birds.

When the birds are just removed from the nest, they will need about 5 feeds every day. The amount of food that each chick eats will differ from the other. When the crop is well rounded, you can feed the birds this formula. This should be done by about 15 days since the eggs hatch.

After 15 days, the temperature of the brooder is reduced to 86 degrees Fahrenheit. You will eliminate one feed but will increase the portion of each feed. This is the schedule and diet that you will maintain until the pin feathers begin to form. This will happen when the birds are about 3 weeks old. They are now ready to be moved into a space at room temperature and are ready for the weaning process and the introduction of new types of foods.

Weaning is the process of getting your bird to eat independently. You can place the foods that you want the bird to consume in a weaning container. Then, all you have to do is lead the birds to the food and wait for them to eat. They may be a little messy initially but will learn to eat well.

The weaning food can include several types of foods like grower pellets, sprouts, fruits and vegetable, small portion of seeds and even dried fruits. They will sample different foods and pick something that they like the most. In the initial phase of weaning the birds, they may not eat too much. So you will have to give them the formula at least thrice a day to make sure that they are not malnourished.

When the birds are fully weaned, they will refuse to eat the formula. This means that they have eaten the food themselves and their crop is too full for any other food. This weaning process cannot be forced upon the birds. Overnight, you will see that the birds have just learned to eat on their own. The time taken to wean completely depends on each individual bird. Providing as many foods as possible during the weaning phase makes the birds less fussy about food. The more variety you are able to add to the diet, the healthier your bird will be. You may notice that the birds will favor seeds over pellets. However, do not get them used to seeds, as they are of no nutritional value to the bird.

Have the hatchlings checked by a vet routinely. He/she will be able to tell you how often they will need a check-up based on the condition of the flock. Getting your hatchlings the necessary vaccines will also keep them healthy and immune to common parrot diseases.

6) Microchipping your bird

This is a great preventive measure against lost birds. You see, our flighted friends have the tendency to get away accidentally. If you leave the cage door open or if you take your bird outdoors, there is always a chance that it will escape. Even if your bird's wings are clipped, the slightest breeze can help your bird get the lift that it needs in order to fly away.

Microchipping will help you track your bird and bring it back in no time. This technology is not restricted to birds. It is used in zoos and also on other pets like dogs. Often rescue shelters have been successful in reuniting pets with their owners because of these microchips.

Microchipping involves inserting a small computer chip under the skin of your bird. This chip is smaller than a rice grain and comes with a unique number that lets you identify your pet. Hypodermic needles are used to inject this chip under the bird's skin. In the case of parrots, the chip is usually inserted in the breast muscle. Make sure you have a qualified vet to do this for you. It is a simple process that does not even need any anesthesia. You will not have to worry about the chip moving around in the body or any moving parts that can cause harm to the bird.

After the chip is inserted you will have to register it with a recovery network for a small one-time fee. All the owner information associated with the unique chip number will be fed into a data base. The fee may vary from $10-25 or £5-10.

The microchip can be used to retrieve information at any given time if your bird is lost. It reduces the chances of your bird being stolen. Some breeders may use leg bands to identify birds. This is not as reliable as it can only be traced by the person who had it inserted in the first place. DNA fingerprinting is an alternative but it is very time consuming and somewhat expensive.

The microchip also allows you to track the gene pool of your bird. If you have a large aviary, you are able to differentiate between two very similar looking birds using the microchip. In some countries, a microchip is mandatory for you to get permits for international travel with your bird.

What you need to take care of is the brand of microchip that you use. Although there are no standards in the manufacturing of microchips, using a popular brand will make it easier for you to read the microchip.

With every microchip you get a scanner. The scanner is normally manufactured by the company that makes the chip. It is not possible for you to read the microchip with any other scanner. So, if you use the chip of a popular company, you are likely to find someone else with a reader or scanner in case you misplace the one that you had. Some of the best brands are InfoPet, PetNet, AVID and Home Again.

When you are registering your pet, it is best to choose a popular network. There are so many networks registering birds that it will become hard for you to look for your bird if you have multiple registrations. Of course, it is also more expensive. Make a note of all the registration details to be sure when the need to recover the information arises.

Microchipping is just an option for pet owners. It is up to you to choose this or any other method of identification. Yet, you need to make sure that your pet has some unique identification tag or chip to locate him/her if they are lost.

7) Looking for a lost parrot

You must have come across several headlines involving birds that were lost or birds that escaped. Sometimes, bird owners can be responsible for these accidents. They may not have kept an eye on the bird to know that the flight feathers have grown back or they may have just become over confident with the training offered to their birds. Of course, leaving doors and windows open is the number one reason for your birds to get away.

Of course, it is also a fact that no matter how careful you are, you cannot control these accidents completely. It is heart breaking to have a pet bird escape. But what is even more heartbreaking is not being able to find your bird because you just do not know how. So, here are a few strategies that you can try to make sure that you get your bird back. Most often, they will be able to help you find your beloved pet.

If you see that your bird is flying away

- Call out your bird's name loudly as it begins to fly. Birds are great at tracking sounds and are likely to get back to you when they hear you.

- Do not look away from your bird and keep your eyes on it for as long as you can. You will be able to tell how far it was able to get, the direction it went in and the possible area that it landed in if you do this.

- Call your friends and family immediately and try to get them to the spot. The more people you have searching for the bird, the easier it will be to find.

Searching for your bird

- Once your friends and family have arrived, look around in the area that you saw the bird last in. You can cover a bigger radius if you have more people looking for the bird.

- There could be several phrases or sounds that your bird is familiar with. Shout them out along with the name of the bird as you are calling out. A lost bird will most likely call back when it hears you. It is definitely afraid and is trying to relocate its flock.

- If you have any recording of your parrot screaming on your phone, play it out. It may respond to this too.

- If your parrot has a mate or a cage mate that it is closely bonded to, take the bird along in a cage and place it in the area that you last saw your parrot in. Stay away from this cage and wait. If the bird in the cage screams or shouts because you are away, the lost bird may respond.

- If you do not find the bird in this area, increase your search radius by 1 mile. It is very unlikely that your parrot would have gone too far away. Only when the wind is too strong or if the bird has been chased by a predator will it get too far from home.

- In many cases, your bird may see you and become absolutely quiet. This is because it feels scared in your presence. So don't just rely on sound or a call back and keep searching for the bird with your eyes.

- Look for movement rather than color. Even with the bright plumes of the Amazon parrot, you just may not be able to see it on a tree or behind bushes.

When you find the bird

If you are lucky enough to find the bird but are unable to reach out to it, there are a couple of things that you can do to get it to come to you:

- The first thing to do would be to relax when you find the bird. If you get overly excited and jumpy, the bird may just fly away. Unless there is any danger around it, just let the bird stay where it is.

- The human that the bird is closest to is the best person to call out to it. You can even bring the bird's cage mate to lure it down.

- Hold out the foods that your bird likes to eat. You can even keep the bird's favorite toy and its food and water bowls out. When it sees something familiar, it is likely that it will fly to it.

- If your bird's wings are clipped, do not urge it to fly down from a very high branch. While it may have gone up there because of the wind, it may not be able to come back down as easily. You may have to get up to the bird and hold the cage or perch out to a place where it will have to take a short flight to reach it.

- Do not raise anything unfamiliar towards the bird. It will definitely back away and get further away from you. It is probably very scared already and will not appreciate anything alien coming towards him/her. If the bird assumes a flight position, stop whatever you are doing.

- Hide from your bird. When it sees that you are gone, it will scream and call out and will try to approach you the moment it sees you again. You will notice the anxiety in your bird as it will start to flutter his/her wings and will also call out to you. The moment you notice this, let him/her see you.

- Do not crowd around the bird's favorite member of the family. Even if he/she wants to fly down, he/she may avoid it because he/she is too scared.

If your bird is still out

If your bird is out even after sun set, you need to make your search a little stronger. This is when your bird will start to settle down or roost. Scream and create a lot of excitement around the bird, as it will make him/her want to fly.

If you cannot reach for the bird, let him/her sleep. You must look around for owls. If there are any traces, they may chase your bird away and you have to either stay put or look for ways to get the bird down. If you are certain that there are no owls, let your bird rest and you can come back for him/her in the morning as he/she is likely to stay in the same place.

If it has been over 24 hours

If you have not managed to spot your bird for 24 hours or more, you may have to seek professional assistance to get your bird. There are a few organizations that you can call for help including:

- The local animal control
- SPCA or the humane society
- Your Vet
- Local zoos
- Pet shops around your area
- The local police.
- You may place an advertisement in the classifieds section of papers.
- You must also constantly check the found section of classifieds to see if anyone has found your bird.
- Post several flyers of the lost bird around the neighborhood.

Never give up hope of getting your bird back. Keep looking for him/her. The good thing is that Amazon parrots love their flock so much that they are among the easiest birds to locate and track. Chances are they may even find their way back home before you know it.

Chapter 7: Amazon Parrot Healthcare

Healthcare is one of the most important aspects of having a pet. With Amazon parrots that are more susceptible to infections than other parrots, you need to take extra care to keep the bird healthy. This chapter will tell you in detail how you can provide great healthcare for your birds and also the common diseases that you need to be aware of.

1) Finding a good avian vet

The first step is to find a reliable avian vet. Avian vets are specialists in dealing with exotic birds. In addition to the general veterinary study, these vets work with exotic birds as part of their initial practice. Most of these vets are also members of the Association of Avian Vets. While it is not mandatory for your avian vet to be a part of the AAV, someone who is a part of it has access to several seminars and conferences conducted by this organization.

It is not very hard to find an avian vet given the popularity of parrots as household pets. However, the biggest challenge that you will face is finding one close to your home. While the regular vets can be approached for emergencies, an avian vet is a must to deal with particular diseases and problems faced by these birds.

The best place to look for a good avian vet in your locality is to check the local yellow pages. Most of the specialized vets are listed here. Of course, the Internet is a reliable source to get all the information that you need with respect to avian vets. The official website of the Association of Avian Vets or www.aav.org will be able to help you locate a good avian vet in your area. The Veterinary Medical Association can be contacted in any part of the world to obtain information about avian vets.

When you do find an avian vet for your bird, make sure that you visit him or her to check out the facility. Once you make this visit, there are a few questions that you must ask him or her to confirm if they are capable of taking care of your bird. Here are a few things you may ask your vet:

- **How much experience do they have with treating birds?** The more time your vet has spent treating birds, the more they are equipped to handle complicated cases. A good background in avian medicine is a must.

- **Have you treated Amazon Parrots before?** The anatomy of birds may be more or less the same. But, the reaction of different birds to various medical procedures can be quite different. Even the symptoms displayed can be very different.

- **Do you have birds at home?** A vet who is also a pet owner will be more sensitive to your bird. They will have a better understanding of the bird's body language and will be able to pick up the most subtle signs that the bird may show during the treatment.

- **Do you have any emergency care provisions?** Your vet should provide some form of after hours care or should have a tie with a veterinary emergency facility. This is to make sure that you can get the right treatment for your bird in case of any emergency.

- **Is he or she willing make house calls?** Sometimes, birds can get really stressed out and will not be able to travel to the facility for treatment. This is especially true in cases of any poisoning or injury that the bird has to deal with. Your vet should be able to provide some sort of house call facility. He or she may personally tend to the bird or should be able to send someone over from the clinic.

- **What are the service costs?** This is the most important question to make sure that you are not caught off guard by exorbitant prices to see your bird. Make sure you get a full rate card that talks about all the services and emergency care fees as well.

- **How often are check-ups recommended?** A good vet will recommend at least one check up every year for your bird. They will tell you in detail what procedures need to be carried out on a regular basis to keep your bird in good shape.

When you are at the vet's also ask for the insurance options for the bird. There are a few insurance plans for birds that will cover a part of the medical care offered to the birds. However, bird insurance is not as perfect as insurance for other pets like dogs or cats. Some of them may even provide third party insurance that covers for any damage caused to other people by your bird. Make sure you check all the clauses of the insurance plan before investing in it.

Most parrot owners prefer to open accounts separately to take care of any emergency medical needs of a bird. A part of their income is set aside in an account every month. This is more reliable than insurance because birds do not have foolproof plans that can keep you prepared for any emergency.

2) Common Amazon parrot diseases

There are different diseases that affect pet birds. In the case of Amazon parrots, most conditions that affect Psittacines will affect them too. In the following section, we will talk about various diseases that affect different parts of the bird.

a) Skin and beak disorders

The common skin and beak problems with Amazon parrots include:

Feather cysts:

Sometimes, the feathers of the birds are unable to grow out through their skin and will curl up under the skin to make a mass as the feather grows. You will notice lumps and swellings on the skin that look somewhat elongated.

Any infection in the feather follicle or any trauma to the skin is responsible for this disorder. You will have to get the follicle surgically removed to ensure that the condition does not occur again in the bird.

Ringworm

This is a condition caused by a fungi called *Cryptococcus*. It normally causes facial dermatitis in parrots. Caged birds may have other skin inflammations caused by fungi and yeast when the cage is not very well maintained.

Parasitic infections

Leg mite and scale face is normally seen in birds. The face and legs develop a mange-like appearance. It normally starts with the formation of crusts around the nostrils, beak and the eyes of the bird. If not treated on time, it can even lead to deformity in the beak of the bird. These crusts may even form on the toes and the legs of the bird. An anti-parasitic medication is prescribed for these conditions that can either be injected or orally administered to the bird.

Psittacine Beak and Feather Disease

This is one of the most common conditions affecting pet parrots. This is caused by a virus called the circovirus. Although the name is beak and feather disease, the condition normally affects only the feathers of the bird and very rarely the beaks.

The first case of this condition was first documented in Cockatoos. Strangely, even these birds only had feather damage despite the disease's name.

This infection is very common in younger birds and is usually seen in birds that are less than 3 years old. The most common signs are feather loss in areas that the bird cannot reach to pluck them out, abnormality in the mature feathers, lack of powder down and also abnormal pin feathers. The infection can spread rapidly, leading to death in most birds before the condition is even diagnosed.

This condition spreads when one bird comes into contact with the feather dust, feces or dander of another affected bird. Most often it is passed on from the adult to the offspring. Even unhygienic nest boxes can be sources of infection.

It is recommended that you isolate a bird that has developed this condition. In worst cases, the birds are euthanized. The problem with this condition is that there is no cure, only preventive care. Making sure that you follow strict quarantining rules, keeping the birds in extremely hygienic spaces and following healthy breeding practices can reduce the chances of the disease spreading within your flock.

Other types of feather damage

Sometimes, your bird will have a very shabby appearance, with the feathers appearing chewed or almost moth-eaten. This may be due to feather plucking, which is common in parrots. However, there are several other causal factors of feather damage in parrots:

- Parasites like red mite, lice and feather mites can cause severe damage to the feathers of the bird.
- Improper nutrition makes the birds less immune to infections and will also affect the function of various organs that are responsible for good skin and feather health.

- Fungus or bacteria from unhygienic cages can lead to infections in the follicle. This type of infection is usually cured with medicines.
- Organ failure, tumor, respiratory conditions and even liver damage can make your bird feel highly stressed. This leads to either self-mutilation or loss of feathers naturally.
- There are various other irritants like tonics that you use on the plumes, ointments, insect bites or even oils that are secreted on human skin that can cause infections. That is why it is recommended that you either use a sanitizer or clean your hands properly before you handle parrots.

b) Nutritional disorders

The diet that your bird follows is one of the most crucial aspects of its health. When you stick to a single source of nutrition like seeds or pellets, you are depriving the bird of several nutrients that can only be obtained from fresh fruits and vegetables. Even fortified bird pellets cannot fulfil the nutritional requirements of birds.

When they do not receive all the nutrients that they require, birds will develop several health issues. You will be able to see specific symptoms for each nutrition-related disease that birds may suffer from.

Today, avian nutrition has seen a lot of improvement as the knowledge about the requirements of bird has also increased tremendously. When you give your bird any food, be very careful about its contents. Very often, the preservatives and dyes used in the foods can adversely affect the bird. Sometimes, when you provide the bird with vitamin supplements in the water, they may not even drink it because of the taste and develop disorders related to dehydration as well. Some of the most common nutritional deficiencies in birds are:

Vitamin A Deficiency

Normally, vitamin A deficiency is unrecognized in birds. It is most common in birds that rely on a diet of nuts and seeds. This kind of a diet lacks most nutrients, especially vitamin A. Of course, if you give your bird too much supplementation of Vitamin A, it can lead to some serious side effects too! The common problems related to excessive Vitamin A are bone abnormalities, liver disease and even reproductive disorders.

There are a few minute signs that you will observe when the bird has a Vitamin A deficiency. These signs depend upon the organ that has been affected. In the earliest stages, you will notice various white spots on the body of the bird. These white spots will eventually become painful abscesses.

They can block the lungs or the respiratory tract of the bird as well. This leads to panting and labored breathing. If left untreated, the bird may even die of suffocation. When the abscess becomes too large, the bird will begin to show a lot of swelling near the eyes. In addition to this, you will notice discharge from the nasal cavity of the bird.

There are other milder symptoms of Vitamin A deficiency as well, including thinness in the plumage, fading of the colors, tail bobbing, lethargy, depression, lack of appetite, bad breath and even gagging.

You can prevent this type of deficiency by ensuring that the diet of your bird is formulated with enough Vitamin A precursors. These precursors are converted into Vitamin A when consumed by the bird. Ask your vet to suggest any vitamin A precursor that is not a potential threat for toxicity.

Never make a supplementation decision on your own. If you are giving your bird a balanced meal but are still seeing these symptoms, consult a vet. Only give the bird the doses of vitamin A as recommended by him. Any excessive dosage can lead to iron storage issues with birds.

Make sure that you include as many natural sources of Vitamin A as you can in your bird's diet. This includes fruits like papaya, cantaloupe, broccoli leaves, turnip leaves, collards, egg yolks, chili peppers, spinach and dandelion greens. They are the safest and most reliable sources of nutrition for your bird.

Iodine deficiency

Goitre is a common condition with birds. The thyroid glands in birds are very small but can enlarge to about thrice their size in the case of any iodine imbalance. The most common signs of iodine deficiency in birds include clicking, wheezing and heavy breathing. Regurgitation may also be observed in some birds. Parrots that are affected with iodine deficiency have very poor tolerance to stress.

You can help your bird by adding supplements like Lugol's iodine in the water that the bird drinks. Using pellets that are fortified with iodine may also work very well with your parrot.

Vitamin D3, Phosphorous or Calcium Imbalance

When your birds are restricted to a seed diet, an imbalance in the phosphorous and calcium ratio is also seen. This leads to a deficiency in the amino acids in the bird's body. The calcium, vitamin D3 and phosphorous ratio is very important because all the vital functions are completed because of this delicate balance.

The biggest problem is providing birds with excessive sunflower seeds because they contain low calcium and amino acid levels. Some pet owners would suggest that you replace sunflower seeds with safflower seeds. This, too, is not the best idea because these seeds are very high in their fat content and may lead to obesity in the bird. They are also equally low in calcium and amino acids.

Vitamin D Toxicosis

While vitamin D is essential to your bird, excessive supplementation causes more harm than good. This leads to an unnatural accumulation of calcium in the kidney and other tissues of the bird's body. Always consult your vet before giving your bird any supplementation.

Iron storage disease

This is a very serious condition that may damage the vital organs of birds, including the liver and the kidney. Every bird's body needs a certain amount of iron to produce the required level of hemoglobin. This is necessary to transfer oxygen from the lungs to the rest of the body. In some cases, however, when the iron build up in the body is excessive, it gets stored in the liver, the heart and the lungs. When stored in these organs, iron can cause a lot of damage.

Iron storage disease comes with almost no signs. You will only notice the health of the bird deteriorate rapidly a few days before it dies. Sometimes, parrot owners are lucky enough to notice signs like a distended abdomen, fluid in the air sacs, labored breathing and fatigue.

Stress and genetic factors also play a rather important role in the development of this condition in birds. This condition is not only related to excessive iron in the diet. If your bird's diet has excessive Vitamin C, iron is absorbed faster into the body. Even an excessive intake of Vitamin A leads to iron storage diseases.

It is best that you avoid nectars fortified with iron, juices, baby foods and other products that contain a lot of iron. Some table scraps can also be harmful to birds as they contain ferrous sulfate, which is even more harmful for your Amazon parrots.

c) Lung and Respiratory disorders
Respiratory and lung disorders in birds are normally caused by fungi, bacteria or parasites. With most of these conditions, treatment is only effective when provided at an early stage of the disease.

Aspergillosis

This is, perhaps, the most common respiratory condition in parrots. There are two forms of this disease. The first type occurs in young birds or birds that have been imported due to the exposure to spores of a fungus called *Aspergillosis*. There is another form of this condition that is more severe. It occurs in birds that live in poorly ventilated areas. Here, the spores are concentrated in these areas and are inhaled into the air sacs of the birds.

Any stress triggers the condition and the bird will begin to show severe symptoms. Vitamin A deficiency is also a trigger for this condition, as it weakens the respiratory system of the bird. Immunity is compromised and the bird develops the chronic form of this condition.

The lower respiratory tract is usually affected by this disease. The trachea, bronchii and the voice organ are also affected along with the air sacs. It is also possible for the infection to spread to other organs from the respiratory tract.

There are a few signs of infection that you will have to watch out for. This includes sudden loss of appetite, strained breathing and inflammation of the air sacs. Death occurs suddenly in most cases because this disease spreads so rapidly.

When the bird is affected by a chronic form of aspergillosis, you will notice fatigue, depression, changes in the voice, labored breathing and even emaciation. The architecture of the respiratory system may also get damaged when the infection becomes too severe.

The only preventive measure against this condition is good hygiene along with a well-balanced diet. You also need to make sure that the cage is well ventilated to avoid any concentration of the fungal spores that are mostly responsible for this condition.

Avian influenza

This is a condition that is usually spread from wild birds to domestic birds. This disease has become a big concern among bird owners simply because it also has the potential to harm human beings in the long run. Several mutations have been observed in this condition, making it more dangerous for human beings.

The Centre for Disease Control and Prevention in the USA has altogether banned any import of birds from certain countries in Asia, Europe and Africa where the disease is prevalent.

This virus is transmitted from one bird to another when they come into contact with each other's feces or respiratory secretion. The most common signs of disease include loss of appetite, swelling of the head, diarrhea, discharge from the eyes and strained breathing. In some cases, the birds may just recover on their own and in other cases, they may die before you are able to notice any symptoms.

Any sign of respiratory diseases requires immediate attention from an Avian vet. You will also have to isolate the bird to ensure that the disease does not spread with the flock.

The disease is usually treated by antibiotics. Vaccines are available to prevent the condition as well. The best way to keep your pet safe is to ensure that there is no contact between your bird and wild birds. Even when you use a piece of wood from the outdoors as a perch for your bird, make sure that it is cleaned perfectly. Any chance of coming into contact with wild birds' environment should be prevented.

d) Kidney related disorders

One of the most common kidney related-conditions in birds is gout. In this condition, an abnormal amount of uric acid crystals accumulate in the body. The liver is responsible for the production of these crystals, while the kidney helps excrete them. However, when the kidney fails to remove these crystal effectively from the bloodstream of the bird, the crystals develop all over the body.

This condition normally occurs when you do not give your bird a balanced meal. If the protein levels are higher than recommended, gout may occur. Too much calcium or very little vitamin A can also cause this condition in birds. Usually, the joint is very badly affected and can be extremely painful.

In conditions where the pain is beyond control with medication, vets opt for euthanasia. The crystals can be removed surgically if they are not very close to the blood vessels. If the proximity is too much, severe bleeding may occur during the surgery, killing the bird.

Oral medicines can be prescribed in the initial stages of the condition. If not treated immediately, gout may even affect the internal organs of the bird. The membranes of most of the vital organs are covered by these crystals, leading to death eventually.

Besides diet, genetics and the environment also play a very important role in the development of gout in birds. This is one of the reasons why regular veterinary examination is a must. If gout is detected early, your bird can be cured with simple medicines and good care.

e) Multi organ diseases

There are several infections that can destroy various parts of your bird's body rapidly when it manifests. These are usually bacterial or viral infections that are quite hard to treat effectively.

Polyomavirus

This is a type of virus that will affect a bird of any age. However, juveniles and hatchlings are most susceptible to this condition. Birds will show a depletion in appetite, sudden weakness, diarrhea and even bruising in the skin or the muscles. This infection usually targets the kidneys, the liver and the heart of the bird. There is very little chance for a bird to survive this infection as it spreads rapidly, leading to death in just 24 to 48 hours.

In a rare case when the bird does survive, there is severe lung and heart damage as well as abnormal feather growth. These birds then become carriers and may spread the condition among the flock.

This virus is spread from the female birds to the egg. Yet, often the infection occurs when a bird comes into contact with the feather dander of an affected bird. There is no treatment available for this condition. The best thing you can do when you detect the symptoms in one of your birds is to isolate it.

Vaccinations are available for hatchlings. You can provide two doses of this vaccine; the first one when the bird is about 4 weeks old and the second one after 2 more weeks. Booster shots are given annually to prevent the condition.

You can also take preventive measures by keeping the cage clean. You need to disinfect the feeders, incubators and even nesting boxes regularly. A vet can help you with the standard procedures of hygiene that can effectively control the manifestation of this disease in birds.

Pacheco's disease

This is a condition that spreads very rapidly in parrots. It is caused by a certain strain of herpes virus. Any stress can lead to a manifestation of symptoms. Birds become more susceptible to this condition under stress, too. It is spread when a bird comes into contact with an affected bird directly. It is also airborne or waterborne. It is common for old world parrots to be carriers of this condition.

The signs of this condition are noticed just days before the bird is about to die. The birds are in great shape with a healthy appetite until then. Suddenly, you will notice fluffing, watery feces and loss of energy in the birds. Very few birds recover from an infection like this.

There are several other herpes virus-related conditions like papillomas that may either be internal or external. In Amazon parrots, internal papillomas are normally noticed. It is believed that these internal papillomas are caused by a virus that is closely related to the Pacheco's disease herpes virus. Another uncommon infection in Amazon parrots is Amazon tracheitis, which is the inflammation of the trachea. This is another condition related to the herpes virus.

Psittacossis

Also known as chlamydiosis, this condition is caused by a bacterial called *Chlamydophiliaa psittaci.* This bacteria is commonly seen in the stool of the infected bird or the nasal secretions of the birds. Since this disease is easily transmitted from birds to people, you need to follow several regulatory practices with respect to quarantining a bird when you bring it home or when it is suspected of having the condition. In many parts of the world, a ban on direct imports of these birds from South America has actually reduced the prevalence of the condition.

In some birds, there is a genetic predisposition to not becoming ill when they are infected. Such birds will remain carriers of the condition though.

The signs of psittacosis usually include depression, ruffled feathers, reduced vocalization or appetite and discharge from the nose and the eyes. In some cases, lime green droppings are also noticed.

There is another form of psittacosis that affects the central nervous system of the bird. In this case, the bird will show signs like twisting of the head, shaking, tremors and even convulsions. While this condition is predominant in old world parrots, you need to make sure that you take enough preventive measures for your Amazon parrot as well.

When this condition has been diagnosed, antibiotics are given to the bird through food or water. Birds that have this condition will require a lot of supportive care. They need to be isolated, given the adequate amount of heat, the absence of stress and of course lots of fluids and good quality food.

Keeping the bird away from potential sources of infection is the best way to prevent the disease. This bacteria will lie dormant for many years and may suddenly manifest when they are stressed. These bacteria are usually found in dry feces. Therefore, regular care and cleaning of the cage is very important. There is always a chance of reinfection if necessary steps are not taken to maintain hygiene.

Remember to protect yourself while handling a sick bird, as you are also susceptible to this condition. Make sure that you wear gloves. After you handle the contents of the cage or the bird, make sure that you thoroughly wash and disinfect your hands. It is necessary, in some states, to report this condition to the local health authorities to coordinate the treatment procedures with the respective government agency.

f) Reproductive disorders

There are always chances of complications and issues when your bird is in breeding season. Reproductive diseases could be recurring or may be prevalent for a few breeding seasons. Some of the most common reproductive diseases in parrots include:

Cloacal prolapse or vent prolapse

The cloaca is that part of the bird where the feces and urine is passed from. The outermost part of this region is called the vent. This vent will control the frequency of droppings in birds. When the inner tissue begins to protrude through the vent, the condition is known as cloacal prolapse or vent prolapse. It is caused by several physiological and psychological conditions that affect the bird. It is necessary to have your bird checked by a veterinarian immediately after you notice the prolapse.

The exact cause of this condition still remains unexplained. It is noticed, however, that it is more common in birds that have been hand raised or have been weaned wrongly. Some birds also have the tendency to hold in their stool, leading to a prolapse.

Surgery and behavior modification are the best remedies to this issue. The hardest part, of course, is modifying the behavior of the bird. In many cases, the close bond between the owner and the bird breaks after the onset of this condition. Sometimes, the bond needs to be broken when the bird has a misplaced sexual emotion towards the owner. This leads to a lot of stress, causing prolapse.

In order to break this bond, the owners must restrict hand feeding, stroking the bird on the back or even holding the bird close to his or her body. If you are unable to change the behavior of the bird, you can look for an animal behavior consultant as well.

Egg binding

Sometimes, the female bird is unable to lay the eggs properly. It is difficult for her to expel the egg. This condition is very common in birds that are overweight. If your bird is not properly stimulated physically and mentally, this condition may occur.

Another common causal factor for this condition is calcium deficiency. Medium to large-sized parrots are very prone to egg binding. Therefore, you need to take extra care of your Amazon parrots during the breeding season.

There are a few signs of egg binding including swaying while walking, unsteady posture, inability to stay up on the perch, wagging of the tail, abdominal swelling etc. Paralysis is also possible if the egg puts any pressure on the nerves of the bird. You must never attempt to remove the egg yourself, as you may end up paralyzing or killing the bird.

When you notice these signs, take the bird to a vet. An X-ray is taken to determine the extent of the condition and to locate the egg in the bird's reproductive tract. There are several methods like hydration, lubrication, additional warmth and calcium supplementation that are used to remove the egg. Abnormalities in the egg will also be tested.

You can provide the bird with various injections like prostaglandins and oxytocin. This will help move the egg along and finally out of the bird. However, when these methods fail, the only option is to remove the egg surgically. Some vets will also try to manually remove the egg if there is no risk of damage caused to the bird's health.

When you notice even a slight deviation from the norm in your bird, consult your vet immediately. This is the key to ensure that your bird is healthier for longer.

g) Cancers and Tumors

Cancers can affect different parts of the bird's body including the lungs, the liver, the ovaries, the various glands and even the stomach. These cancers are removed surgically and are treated with chemotherapy as well. Some of the most common types of tumors in birds include:

- Squamous cell carcinomas or skin cancers that you will notice around the beak and the eyes, the toes and the wings. Radiation therapy is recommended for these birds. Some skin tumors called fibrosarcomas are also seen on the skin of the bird in the form of red dots.

- Lipomas are fatty tumors that will be seen near the breast bone and the chest area of the bird. These tumors are usually benign and are not removed unless they put any pressure on the organs of the bird.

- Xanthomas are yellow masses that are normally seen under the skin of the bird. They affect the breast bone, the tips of the wings and the chest. This is a common sight in many species of pet birds. The cause of this is unknown, although most studies relate it to poor nutrition that leads to Vitamin A deficiency. These tumors are also benign. However, they tend to bleed profusely as they grow bigger in size.

- Lyphoma is a common occurrence in most pet animals. It is treated with chemotherapy and radiation just like other pets.

- Pituitary adenomas are commonly seen in parrots. They are an acute condition that affect the nervous system of the bird. Muscle spasms and seizures are common in birds that are affected with this condition. Some of the most common signs of this condition are excessive urination and excessive thirst.

h) Behavioral problems
Mental health is one of the most important aspects of parrot healthcare. As mentioned before, these birds are extremely intelligent and highly analytical. If they are not mentally stimulated or if they feel bored or lonely, they may develop several behavioral issues.

These issues compromise the well-being of the bird, as they may get into fights, may stop eating or may even mutilate themselves in the pursuit of seeking attention. Some of the common behavioral problems are:

Excessive screaming

Amazon parrots are noisy. You can expect them to scream in the morning or after sunset as instinctive behavior. A quiet parrot is a myth. But, screaming can become an issue when the bird does this as a means of seeking attention. If you notice that your bird screams every time you leave the room, it is a sign that your bird has some behavioral disorder.

Now, the most crucial thing is how you respond to this behavior. It will determine whether your bird will continue to scream and shout or whether it will learn to control its behavior.

There are a few dos and don'ts when you notice that your bird has become excessively noisy:

- Never respond to the bird's screams. If you respond with a "no!" or a "stop it", your bird will feel encouraged to scream. It does not see it as a negative response. All he/she sees it as is a call back from you.

- When the bird screams as soon as you leave the room, do not come back. Wait for the bird to calm down and become quiet. Return to the bird only when you know that it is fully calm. This tells the bird that it will get your attention only with good behavior.

- Whenever you leave the room, give your bird treats and toys. The more positive experiences it has when you leave, the more independent it will become.

Think of the different types of attention that you can give your bird. Make sure that your bird gets a little of everything. That way, it is independent and will not depend on you for all the entertainment and recreation.

Aggression

An aggressive bird is one that nips and bites whenever you approach it. If your bird becomes aggressive all of a sudden, it means that it is going through some sort of stress. It could be that your bird is becoming hormonal and is craving a mate.

If the bird is injured or in pain, it may become aggressive and could bite often. You can also look around to see if there are any objects that are disturbing the bird. Objects that are too colorful or that make noise can upset the bird. Remove these items from the room and see how your bird behaves. If it continues to be nippy, consult your vet. This is if your bird develops these habits suddenly.

However, some birds are naturally more aggressive than others. This behavior can be altered with proper training. In many cases, aggressive behavior is not really to cause harm or to keep you away. Biting is your bird's way of seeking attention. It is trying to get you to respond or pay attention to it. So, you can even take this as a sign of boredom and loneliness in the bird. There are a few things you can do to prevent this behavior in birds:

- Do not respond. All your bird wants is your attention. Even if the bite is extremely painful and you just want to shout, control it. When your bird hears a scream or any other response, it is encouraged to continue this behavior.

- A popular method is called the "earthquake" method. If the bird is on your hand and begins to bite, just shake your hand a little like a tremor. An unsteady perch is the most unpleasant thing for a parrot. It will stop biting immediately. If it is on your shoulder or your head and begins to nibble at your ear, just run with him/her still perched on you. This will also be very unpleasant to the bird and it will respond by stopping this behavior.

- You can even put the bird back in the cage when it bites. Separation from you is also an unpleasant experience for your bird. If it realizes that biting makes you unhappy, it is a behavior it will try to control.

- Lastly, press your bird's head down whenever it bites and softly say "No!" This is an uncomfortable position for the bird. If you do this every time it bites, it will definitely stop this type of behavior with time.

When you associate negative experiences with behavior that you do not want from your bird, you can expect it to stop it. It takes a few attempts for your bird to make that association. Be consistent with your training. If you let the bird get away with this behavior and then stop it the next time, he/she will just get confused.

Feather plucking

This is one of the most unpleasant behaviors in birds. Birds will lose their feathers seasonally in a process called molting. Then, new feathers will just grow back in their place. The bird may be a little irritable in this phase but a bit of misting will calm it down. This is a natural, seasonal process. However, feather plucking is a voluntary behavior that leads to self-mutilation. Your bird will voluntarily pluck its feathers off, leaving bald patches. Sometimes, the bird may even develop scabs and wounds on the body due to excessive plucking.

There are many physical and psychological factors that lead to feather plucking in birds. Some of the common causal factors are:

- Stress and boredom
- Liver disease
- Allergies
- Cancer
- Internal or skin parasites
- Infectious diseases

- Nutritional disorders
- Heavy metal poisoning
- Low humidity
- Less sunlight
- Lack of fresh air

One of the most common factors is malnutrition. If your bird is on a seed only diet, it will not get the nutrition he/she needs. This leads to feather abnormalities which eventually leads to plucking and mutilation. Some of the preservatives in the foods that you give your bird may also cause these allergic reactions.

When you suspect feather plucking, contact your vet immediately to have the condition diagnosed properly. You can make a few changes to the bird's immediate environment to reduce feather plucking:

- Make sure that your bird gets at least 12 hours of light and darkness every day. You can cover the cage with a blanket to give him/her enough resting time.

- Give your bird a lot of attention. Schedule your day in such a way that you get at least 20 minutes to play and interact with your bird every day. Try to schedule one time for this interaction. That makes your bird look forward to this routine and will reduce anxiety.

- Give your bird lots of toys. That helps to keep it distracted. Whenever your bird has free time, give him/her a foraging toy to engage his/her mind. Rearranging chewing and climbing toys within the cage is a lot of fun for the bird. It will keep their interest in the toys.

- Check for any triggers in your bird's environment whenever it plucks. If there is any object or person that stimulates this behavior in your bird, keep them away from your bird.

- Giving your bird a bath regularly works very well. Simple misting on a daily basis gives your bird a feeling of being in the rain forest. Wet feathers also promote grooming and preening in birds. This is very relaxing for them and they will voluntarily reduce the amount of plucking over time.

- Try to include new foods in your bird's diet. This will make him/her gain more interest in the routine. Try spray millet, cereal, bean mix or even some pasta.

- If any stressful situation is making your bird pluck, avoid those situations. For example, some birds hate being stroked. If you see it pluck when you stroke him/her, stop immediately.

- Do not let the bird think that you are a mate. Then, in the breeding season, the bird becomes exceedingly irritable and will display a lot of feather plucking. Actions like stroking the back, under the wings etc. will make the bird hormonal in the breeding season. This makes the bird pluck its feathers in frustration.

- You need to take your bird to the vet regularly. Follow up care is necessary for a bird that has displayed feather plucking in the past. There are several treatments that can prevent this behavior in your bird. You may also have to administer medicines and supplements to your bird to reduce the problem of plucking.

Usually, feather plucking is not seen in the wild. This is because birds are occupied all day looking for food, staying away from predators, maintaining their status as predators etc. The primary reason for this behavior in captivity is boredom, according to research conducted on parrots.

Sometimes, even the best kept Amazon parrots will display this sort of behavior. It is actually quite a hard behavioral pattern to understand. For some owners, a simple change in the environment helps the birds and for others even the most extensive treatment does not help. It is, therefore, necessary to seek medical attention for your bird at the slightest display of this behavior. Omega 3 fatty acids are known to help the bird in some rare cases. If nothing works, you may even take your bird to an animal behavior consultant who can tell if there are any underlying psychological factors that are triggering this behavior in your bird.

3) Injuries and accidents

There are several accidents and injuries that birds are susceptible to. They may get into fights with one another, fly into windows or even suffer from poisoning. These are emergencies that you have to deal with immediately. But first, you need to identify what is causing distress to your birds in the first place. Here are some common accidents in birds:

Heavy metal poisoning

Metals like zinc and lead are common in our environment. That is why you need to take extra care to ensure that your birds do not get exposed to them for long. It is best that you never let your bird outside the cage without any supervision. You must also carefully inspect the bird's environment and make sure that there are no sources of these heavy metals like fencing and even the cage material around the bird. Selecting the cage material carefully is one of the best preventive measures against metal poisoning.

Zinc poisoning is more common than lead poisoning because of the process of galvanization that has become so popular today. This is used in the construction of wiring material and even the cage itself. As for lead, the common sources are lead weights used in fishing, curtain weights, stained glass, old paint etc.

Excessive thirst, depression, weakness and regurgitation of water are the most common signs of heavy metal poisoning in birds. In some cases lack of coordination, excessive trembling and even seizures are observed.

An X-ray of the bird is taken to determine the presence of any metals in the gizzard of the bird. Blood tests are also required to check for any metal in the blood stream. Medication called chelating agents are given to the bird along with supportive care when poisoning is detected. This is usually injected into the bird's muscle. When the bird is stable, you can even administer this agent orally. The response to treatment is usually quite rapid, provided that it is not too severe.

Fume or aerosol poisoning

Overheating surfaces that contain Teflon, Tefzel and Silverstone can release fumes that are toxic for birds. Most nonstick cookware, self-cleaning ovens and irons have a coating of fluropolymers. This material will begin to release particles when heated slightly. The particles that are released are toxic for the birds.

Besides this, there are various other chemical hazards in our homes that can affect the birds. Aerosol products including deodorants, carpet fresheners, room fresheners, oven cleaners and other substances like plastic can be sources of irritants and toxins for birds. Smoke is one of the most dangerous things for the birds in your home.

The common signs of fume or aerosol poisoning include neurological symptoms like tremors, labored breathing and even sudden death. Normally, even the slightest exposure is deadly for the bird, giving the owner no time to get the bird away from the environment. It is best to be cautious and make sure that your bird's cage is placed in such a way that it is not close to any sources of these toxic fumes. The cage should also be in a room that is very well ventilated to prevent any accumulation of these toxins.

Fractures

Broken bones and dislocations are quite common among pet birds. The problem with the bones in birds is that they are filled with air and are actually part of the respiratory system of the bird. In addition to that, the bones are also quite brittle, leading to multiple fractures when the bird has an accident.

If you notice that your bird has a dislocated wing or broken wing, it is best not to touch the bird. Contact your vet immediately to prevent any further damage. He/she will be able to guide you through the process of stabilizing the bone of your beloved pet. Rigid stabilization is good enough in most cases, as bird bones heal rather quickly. Only in extreme conditions will surgery be required to restore the normal function of the bones that are affected.

Physical therapy is also recommended for birds with broken bones. This is to ensure that the joints do not become frozen and stiff, reducing the range of motion of the area. An orthopedic specialist is usually recommended to help your bird recover faster.

4) First aid kit for parrots

Having a first aid kit ready for your parrot will help you take care of emergencies like bleeding or bruises before taking the bird to the vet. Accidents are quite common with pet birds and it is up to you to make sure that you are always prepared. Your parrot first aid kit must contain:

- **Important phone numbers:** Have the number of your vet ready along with an alternative number. You may also want to keep the number of your nearest emergency clinic.

- **Flour:** Flour helps control any bleeding on the bird's body. You can alternatively get a styptic stick to do the same.

- **Tweezers or hemostats:** These are also called forceps in common terms. They help you handle the tiny bandages and plasters that you will have to use on the bird.

- **Scissors:** You can use scissors for a host of different activities like trimming the feathers, cutting bandages etc.

- **Cotton swabs and gauze pads:** They also help control any bleeding. In addition to that, you can also clean wounds using these cotton swabs.

- **Bandage material:** You will need pressure wraps on cuts and fractures. For this you need good material that will not stick to the feathers of the birds. Cellophane, masking tape and roll gauze are your best options.

- **Disinfectants:** You will have to clean open wounds with disinfectants. The most reliable ones are hydrogen peroxide and dilute chlorhexidine. Petroleum jelly, salves and ointments that are thick and jelly-like should always be avoided.

- **A syringe:** Flushing small wounds is necessary. You can get a 3 mm syringe for this purpose. It is also used to provide oral medication for birds that are injured or unwell.

- **Restraining towel:** A clean washcloth will help you handle a distressed bird easily. Make sure that it doesn't have loops or threads that the toe may get stuck in.

With these materials, you have a basic first aid kit in place. You can add a heating pad and a thermometer as well. These items are especially useful during the breeding and nesting period.

5) Preventive healthcare

Prevention is always better than cure. Here are a few preventive measures that you can take to ensure that your bird is always healthy:

- Keep the cage clean: Damp and dirty surfaces are breeding grounds for several fungi and bacteria. Infections can be prevented by cleaning the cage and its contents regularly.

- Provide good nutrition: A balanced meal that contains pellets and also natural food sources like nuts, fruits and vegetables can prevent several deficiency-related issues in birds.

- Make sure your bird gets enough exercise: Boredom can lead to a lot of stress in birds, making them susceptible to various disorders.

- Quarantine new birds: When you are sure that your new bird is healthy, you can introduce it to the rest of the flock. The fact that human beings are also susceptible to conditions affecting birds makes it necessary to quarantine them properly.

- Regular veterinary check-ups: The best way to make sure that your bird is not carrying any infection or disease is to have a qualified vet check the bird regularly. You need to make sure that your bird gets a thorough check up at least once a year.

With these preventive measures, you should be able to control most diseases that affect Amazon parrots. In any case, an Amazon parrot is a hardy bird that holds up well against most of these diseases. However, keeping an eye on the bird and spending quality time with him/her will help you notice any behavioral changes or issues. The earlier you address these problems, the easier is the treatment process.

6) What to do if your bird is hospitalized

There may be times when you have to get your bird hospitalized. In the case of extreme injuries, surgeries or even during the recovery phase of certain diseases your bird will be kept in the hospital. Having a pet in the hospital can be a very overwhelming experience. Here are a few tips to deal with this situation in the most practical way possible:

- Make sure you communicate with your veterinarian effectively. He/she should be able to help you with all the information that you need with respect to the pace of recovery of your bird or the requirements for your bird to get better soon.

- Ask your vet to help you out with some contact details of another staff member. This will help you have some point of contact when you need information immediately. Sometimes, the vet may be tending to another patient and may be unavailable to tend to you right away.

- Have one person in your family as the point of contact always. This is easier for the hospital as well.

- When you plan on visiting your pet, make sure you give the facility a call before you do so. Sometimes, a facility may request you not to do so. This is because pets get excited when they see their owners. This may interfere with the process of recovery of your bird. In other cases, your bird may need your presence in order to get better faster.

- The length of stay and the possible recovery period is decided upon by the veterinarian who is taking care of your bird. Your bird may just be placed in a separate cage if the condition is not too severe. If it is severe, however, the bird may be required to stay in the ICU or in isolation.

- Food, water and other needs of your bird are taken care of by the hospital. They will have staff that is available on a 24/7 basis to help take care of your bird.

Birds are monitored regularly to ensure that they are in good enough condition to leave the hospital. The heart rate, the rate of respiration, the oxygen reaching the body and other bodily functions are checked thoroughly.

The reason birds are hospitalized in most cases is to make sure that timely help may be provided in cases where there is any other abnormality that is detected during the process of recovery.

When your pet is ready to be taken home, you will be notified. Then, if you have other birds at home, it may become necessary to quarantine your bird for a brief period. The required care after hospitalization will be explained to you in detail when you are getting your pet discharged from the hospital.

7) Caring for a bird after surgery

With surgeries come stitches and wounds. For a bird, this is only a hinderance and he/she may try to peck at it and will end up making the wound worse. Besides that, the care requirements of the bird change drastically when he/she comes home after surgery.

First, check the sleep cycle of the bird. He/she may be sleeping more and may be a little drowsy because of painkillers or sedatives. If this persists for several days, it is an indication of some issue.

Second, your bird's appetite may either fall drastically or he/she may want to eat a lot of food. Usually it is the former. This is when you reduce the food given to the bird or you may only give the bird food when he/she shows signs of hunger. This appetite will return to normal quite soon. Make sure that the bird has a lot of water to drink in this phase.

As mentioned before, your bird will try to bite or lick the wound. This should always be discouraged. One of the best ways to prevent this is to get a small Elizabethan collar, which looks like a plastic cone around the bird's head. This will be available at your vet.

You need to make sure that the wound is checked twice every day. During this time, the wound should always be kept dry. If you notice any swelling, irritation, heat or bad odor from this region, contact your vet immediately.

If the bird is wearing a bandage, have it cleaned and changed regularly. Any debris or dirt on this bandage can cause severe infections.

If you have any doubt about your bird's health, do not hesitate to consult a doctor immediately. They will be available to take care of any query or emergency for you.

Conclusion

Thank you for buying this book. Here is hoping that the book was able to answer all the queries that you could possibly have as an Amazon parrot owner.

It is true that caring for these birds can be quite a challenge. However, with pet owners like you who are eager to learn more and give their bird the best, there is no doubt that the bird will have a safe and comfortable home.

If you found the information in this book useful and practical, let other pet owners know, too. Leave a comment about the book and tell us what made it a helpful tool in raising your parrot.

Here's to several years of joy and companionship with your doting parrot friend.

References

You need to keep yourself updated with all the information available about Amazon parrots. Of course, the Internet is the best place to look, as it is loaded with interesting forums, blogs and websites that can provide you with all the info you need about Amazon parrots. You will even get to interact with parrot owners who have dedicated their lives to providing a loving home for their feathered friends.

Note: at the time of printing, all the websites below were working. As the internet changes rapidly, some sites might no longer live when you read this book. That is, of course, out of my control.

Here are a few links that you can refer to:

www.gopetsamerica.com
www.webvet.com
www.pets4homes.co.uk
www.beautyofbirds.com
www.birds.about.com
www.birdchannel.com
www.buffalolib.org
www.animal-world.com
www.parrotparrot.com
www.petsuppliesplus.com
www.parrot-and-conure-world.com
www.parrotparrot.com
www.cutagulta.com
www.faze.ca
www.goodbirdinc.com
www.shadypines.com
www.studentswithbirds.wordpress.com
www.dummies.com
www.howcast.com
www.funtimebirdy.com
www.associationofanimalbehaviorprofessionals.com
www.pets.thenest.com
www.gopetsamerica.com

www.northernparrots.com
www.companionparrots.org
www.indianringneck.com
www.jamiesparrothelp.wordpress.com
www.defenders.org
www.forums.avianavenue.com
www.parrotdebate.com
www.merckvetmanual.com
www.petcareandshare.co
www.forthebirdsdvm.com
www.drsfostersmith.com
www.hartz.com
www.belizebirdrescue.com
www.fws.gov
www.environment.nsw.gov.au
www.peta.org
www.companionparrotonline.com
www.birding.about.com
www.animal-world.com
www.petfinder.com
www.aav.org
www.cites.org
www.sevenparrots.com
www.trainedparrot.com
www.scottemcdonald.com
www.parrotbreeding.com.au
www.cicerovet.com

www.ingramcontent.com/pod-product-compliance
Lightning Source LLC
LaVergne TN
LVHW021522080426
835509LV00018B/2603